P9-CKY-240

Make Your Own Musical Instruments

Muriel Mandell & Robert E. Wood

Sterling Publishing Co., Inc.   New York

OTHER BOOKS OF INTEREST

Best Singing Games for Children of All Ages
Cheerleading & Songleading
Dancing Games for Children of All Ages
Family Book of Crafts
Gospel Music Encyclopedia
Holiday Singing and Dancing Games
Movement Games for Children of All Ages
Musical Games for Children of All Ages
Silly Songbook
Singing and Dancing Games
Singing & Dancing Games for the Very Young
Whittling & Wood Carving

Copyright © 1957 by Sterling Publishing Co., Inc.
Two Park Avenue, New York, N.Y. 10016
Distributed in Australia by Oak Tree Press Co., Ltd.
P.O. Box K514 Haymarket, Sydney 2000, N.S.W.
Distributed in the United Kingdom by Blandford Press
Link House, West Street, Poole, Dorset BH15 1LL, England
Distributed in Canada by Oak Tree Press Ltd.
℅ Canadian Manda Group, 215 Lakeshore Boulevard East
Toronto, Ontario M5A 3W9
Manufactured in the United States of America
All rights reserved
Library of Congress Catalog Card No.: 57-11535
Sterling ISBN 0-8069-5022-6 Trade
5023-4 Library
7658-6 Paper
First Paperback Printing 1982

Contents

1. THE FASCINATION OF MAKING YOUR
   OWN INSTRUMENTS 7

2. RHYTHM STICKS, BLOCKS AND SCRAPERS 9
   City Slicker Sticks . . . Country Style Sticks . . . Claves . . .
   Minstrel Bones . . . Sandpaper Sticks . . . Notched Stick
   . . . Rhythm Blocks . . . Sandpaper Blocks . . . Chinese
   Wood Block . . . Coconut Halves . . . Washboard Morache
   . . . American Indian Morache . . . Grater Guayo . . .
   Plywood Guiros.

3. SHAKERS AND RATTLES 16
   Tin Can Tubo . . . Clothespin Chatterboxes . . . Bone
   Rattle . . . Papier Mache Maracas . . . Seashell Shakers . . .
   Coconut Rattles . . . Gourd Rattle . . . Bull-Roarer . . .
   Rattles from This and That.

4. CASTANETS, TRIANGLES, CYMBALS 27
   Pop Top Castanets . . . Walnut Castanets . . . Triangles
   . . . Cymbals . . . Jingle Clogs . . . Jingle Ring . . . Jangle
   Ring.

5. BELLS, CHIMES AND MARIMBAS 34
   Sleigh Bells . . . Bell Bracelets . . . Bell Stick . . . Train
   Bells . . . Flower Pot Bells . . . Stone Bells . . . Chimes . . .
   Marimba or Xylophone . . . One-Octave Marimba.

6. DRUMS, DRUMS, DRUMS 44
   Tin Can Tomtoms . . . Mixing Bowl Drum . . . Basket
   Drum . . . Cheesebox Hoop . . . Tambourines . . . Drum-
   sticks of Sorts.

7. SKIN DRUMS 57
   Skin Drumheads . . . Barrel Conga . . . Coconut Drums . . .
   Variable Pitch Coconut Drum . . . Coconut Bongos . . .
   Fiber Pipe Drum Set . . . Stove Pipe Drum . . . Drum
   Set Frame.

8. ODDS AND ENDS FOR RHYTHM BANDS 76
   Salt Box Drum . . . Band Box Drum . . . Scraping Screw
   . . . Ten-Penny Triangle . . . Paper Bag Maracas . . . Brad
   Bells . . . String Bass . . . Kettle Drum . . . Coat Button
   Castanets . . . Basket Stem Bell . . . Pot Cover Gong . . .
   Button Ankle Rattles . . . Hot Tin Can . . . Triangle Forks
   . . . Temporary Tambourine . . . Whisk Broom Swish . . .
   Spoon Syncopators . . . Wooden Spoon Rhythm.

9. STRINGS 82
   Tuber Harp . . . Wishbone Harp . . . Slingshot Strummer
   . . . Urban Slingshot Strummer . . . Shoebox Strummer . . .
   Box Banjo . . . Wire Hanger Harp . . . Washtub Bass . . .
   Can Contralto . . . My-olin.

10. BLOW, MEN, BLOW 96
    Bottle Flute . . . Key Whistle . . . Corn Stalk Whistle . . .
    Soda Straw Pipe . . . Sea Shell Blower . . . Pipes of Pan
    . . . Test Tube Pipes . . . Comb Kazoo . . . Humboard
    Kazoo . . . Willow Whistle . . . Rubber Hose Recorder . . .
    Bass Rubber Hose Recorder . . . Papoose Pipe.

11. CLAY 111
    Tips on Clay . . . Clay Drum . . . Clay Bell . . . Clay
    Maracas.

12. HOW TO MAKE LIKE A MUSICIAN 118
    The Band or Orchestra . . . Instruments with Make-
    Believe . . . Instrument Games for Two or More.

Index 127

Photo by Ben Rose Studios

Making like musicians — with home-made instruments. Teacher Bob Wood plays on a rubber hose recorder as students at New Lincoln Schools, New York City, follow with recorder, my-olin, wire hanger harp, tin can tubo and coconut drum. In the background are sets of fiber pipe drums and flower pot bells.

1. The Fascination of Making Your Own Instruments

As you create your own musical instruments and play them, you not only have fun, but you also add to your understanding of music. You may have played a flute, for instance, without realizing that you produced your high notes by shortening the pipe. In the process of making your own flute, you are certain to learn this and other principles of music making.

Don't try to swallow this book as a whole. Taste each portion that appeals to you as you browse through it. Then select those instruments which excite your curiosity and make them.

First come the percussion instruments (played by "striking") since they require the least musical knowledge. The rhythm sticks and blocks, the scrapers and shakers, the castanets, cymbals and triangles, the bells, the drums and the tambourines are fine for beating out patterns of heavy and light beats — to accompany dancing or singing or the melody-making of phonograph, radio or television set. Toward the end of this percussion section are the percussion "melody" instruments on which tunes can be made. These include the musical glasses, the flower pot bells, the marimba (or xylophone) and the drums with more than one note. Each can be tuned to scales or ladders of sound.

Following the percussions are the instruments of the string family. These are graduated from the strictly-for-fun rubber band instruments to the melodious and instructive washtub bass and "my-olin." Similarly, the chapter on the wind family leads up to the recorder, which is a challenge to make and play.

The separate section on clay instruments is included for those who have facilities for firing or hardening the clay.

Read through all of the varieties of a particular type of instrument before you start constructing any. Each project is written up in some detail, with the simplest version of each musical instrument given first. These instruments are to show you what can be done and what has been done by other young musicians. In a sense, these are a call to your own imagination and inventiveness and are really only examples of the kind of thing you can make up yourself. You can create your own instruments by varying the materials, sizes, etc. Many musical instruments came into being because the country in which they developed had a ready supply of a material — bamboo, gourds, silk or metals.

Such collections as "Odds and Ends for Rhythm Bands," (page 76) and "Rattles from This and That," (page 24) are meant to serve as springboards for other ideas. Look around you. You can unearth the raw materials for musical treasures from the kitchen and the bathroom, the butcher and the baker, the garage and the junkyard, the woods and the seashore.

After you and your friends have each made an instrument or two, it is time to enjoy them. In "How to Make Like a Musician," there are suggestions for experimenting with the instruments, for grouping them in duets and trios, for forming an orchestra and for making the musical instruments part of your play acting and dancing. Finally, there are several games to play with your instruments.

You will notice that no music is supplied except for a few samples to help construct and practice with some of the melody instruments. When you are ready to play, there are any number of fine song books you can follow on your homemade instruments.

2. Rhythm Sticks, Blocks and Scrapers

To tap out patterns of heavy and light sounds, anything from two pencils to two brush handles can be made into rhythm sticks. It's easy to make a pair that will look and sound just right when clicked together. Rhythm sticks are fun to move to — for walking, marching, running, leaping, galloping, gliding or skipping.

CITY SLICKER STICKS

It is easy to make rhythm sticks out of dowels. Dowels are round sticks of wood, usually birch or maple. They can be bought 3/16 of an inch to one inch in diameter. Used normally in furniture construction, dowels are sold by your hardware man. A 3-foot length of 1/2-inch doweling costs about 10 cents.

Rhythm sticks should measure about 12 inches long. So saw your 3-foot doweling into three parts. Then smooth down the saw cuts with sandpaper and round the edges.

You can coat your rhythm sticks with shellac or varnish, or paint them an attractive color.

COUNTRY STYLE STICKS

Choose your wood from the trunk of a hardwood sapling — birch, maple or striped maple. The wood from the trunk of a young tree will be stronger than that from the branch of a larger tree. Saw off a section one inch in diameter and about a foot long.

Strip off the bark while the wood is freshly cut. Then to get the best tone, allow the wood to dry several days.

With a hatchet or an ax, split your wood lengthwise. Whittle your sticks or use a rasp and single-cut file until you have made them round. Sandpaper them smooth.

Rub them lightly with linseed oil or shellac, varnish or paint.

CLAVES

Calypso and Spanish claves are wider and shorter than most rhythm sticks. Get the one-inch doweling for these and don't make them longer than 8 inches.

Coat them with a dark finish.

To play, cup one in your hand and hit it across the top with the other.

MINSTREL BONES

Make sure you have short ribs of beef for supper and rescue two of the bones.

Nibble off or cut off all the meat. Then wash them clean with plenty of hot water and soap and a brush. Dry the bones well, preferably in the sun.

Play them as you do claves by cupping one in your hand and hitting it across the top with the other bone. Or grasp two bones between index and middle finger of one hand and tap out rhythm by shaking your hand. The wonderful resonance will surprise you.

SANDPAPER STICKS

Wrap rough sandpaper around 12-inch lengths of dowel (one inch wide). Tack or glue them in place. Scrape the dowels back and forth across each other.

NOTCHED STICK

For a different rhythm, make a notched stick. Start with a 12-inch length of ½-inch doweling. A coping saw and chisel are the handiest tools for the job.

Beginning 2 inches from one end of the stick, make circular grooves ⅛ of an inch deep and ⅛ of an inch apart. Make saw cuts and gently slit out the wood between the cuts with the help of a chisel.

Chisel out similar grooves until about 3 inches of your stick is notched.

The notched stick is played by coupling it with a plain stick of the same size. (One of your rhythm sticks is exactly right.) Hold the notched stick in your left hand, and rub the other stick over the notches.

RHYTHM BLOCKS

Any scrap of wood can be cut into rhythm blocks as long as you can cut two blocks of the same size; but it is easier to play with blocks less than an inch thick. Use a cross-cut saw, and make your blocks square, round, oblong or triangular. Sand them smooth. Then shellac or paint them if you wish.

You'll need handles, and this will give you a chance to be original. You can use drawer pulls, strips of an old leather belt, pot cover handles, spools, narrow blocks of wood, etc.

SANDPAPER BLOCKS

From scrap wood or a heavy box slat ½ to ¾ of an inch thick, cut two blocks about 6 inches long and 4 inches wide. Cover the bottom and sides of each block with a sheet of sandpaper (sand side up), tacking it down with heavy tacks or large-headed nails. The surfaces of the sandpaper when rubbed together will give you the shuffling sound you want.

For each block, use a hardwood handle about 5 inches long and 1¾ inches wide, attaching it with 2-inch screws. Or make handles of drawer pulls, leather straps or empty spools.

Decorate the top with a coat of paint.

Shuffle off to rhythm.

CHINESE WOOD BLOCK

Would you ever expect to get sounds of galloping horses and tramping feet out of a Chinese wood block? You can! Make one from a deep wooden cigar box or an oblong cheese box. Get your drill and saw ready.

Stand your box on end with the cover closed. On each of the four long sides, bore a ¼-inch hole about 2 inches down from the top. With a keyhole saw, carefully work from the holes and cut slits about 4 or 5 inches long and ¼ of an inch wide. Smooth the edges with sandpaper.

Drill two holes in one end of the box for a handle of heavy cord or rope. Knot each end of the rope on the inside of the box. Nail or tape the cover down securely.

You can finish the box with a coat of dark stain and a coat of shellac or varnish. Don't use paint because it muffles the sound.

Beat out your parade and cowboy sound effects with a drumstick made from a stick with its bead wrapped in cotton (see page 53).

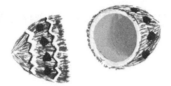

COCONUT HALVES

Use a sharp saw to cut a coconut in half. Drain out the milk, pry out the meat and clean the inside thoroughly. Sand the edges smooth. Paint or shellac both inside and outside.

See how many different sounds you can make, besides just clapping them together.

Tap the two halves lightly together in rhythm. Does it sound like galloping over ice?

Try placing a sheet of paper between the two coconut halves and rubbing in time to music. Does it sound like walking through snow?

WASHBOARD MORACHE

Ask Mom for her old washboard. In addition, persuade her to let you raid her sewing box for thimbles. You may have to borrow a few from a neighbor, but maybe her children would like to play, too. You need five thimbles.

Put the thimbles on the fingers of one hand. Hold the washboard with your other hand and cradle it against your chest. Run the thimbled fingers up and down the ridges of the board. The particular sound you make will depend on the size of the board and on the material of which it is made. But the rhythms you tap out will be fine for singing, marching, dancing or just listening.

AMERICAN INDIAN MORACHE

With a little jackknife skill, you can make an American Indian scraping instrument and play it with your rhythm or jazz band.

You'll need two sticks — one to hold, the other for scraping.

Choose a branch or a piece of scrap wood about half an inch thick and 2 inches wide. It can be 12 to 24 inches long. Thin down one side with your knife and whittle open notches half an inch wide, spacing them every half inch or so. Round all edges with sandpaper.

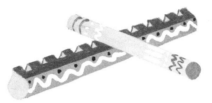

For use as a scraper, round out another stick from 8 to 10 inches long and ¾ of an inch thick. You can use ¾-inch doweling.

Of course, you can carve, stain or paint both sticks.

To play, place one end of the notched stick on an inverted bread basket or metal dishpan. Hold the other end in your left hand. Rub the scraping stick up and down rhythmically.

GRATER GUAYO

After meal preparation is finished, you can find extra work for the potato grater. Try scraping it in time to music with a thimbled finger or a fork. For variety of sound, enlist all sides of the grater (including the masher section, if your grater has one).

You may like a wooden scraper better than the thimble or fork. You can use a pencil or toy hammer, or a toy rod and bead.

PLYWOOD GUIROS

Plywood is now sold with grooves cut on the flat side. It is called striated plywood. Use it as is. You can make the sound louder and more resonant by nailing a piece on top of a wooden cigar box.

Play your plywood with thimbled fingers, nail file or wooden rod.

3. Shakers and Rattles

TIN CAN TUBO OR SHAKER

For your Latin American tunes, you'll need this one. It's a variation of the old Indian rattle, and you can make a tubo very much like those offered in the stores.

For this exotic shaker, find two tin cans of the same size. Remove the contents but don't entirely remove the covers so you can push them back into place later. Scrape off the labels under hot water.

Into one can, throw a half dozen kernels of rice or dry cereal or a cupful of sand. Into the other, put several paper clips, nails, pebbles or bottle caps. Reseal at least one of the cans, with scotch tape if necessary. Bind the two cans together with adhesive tape.

Paint an interesting design with enamel on the cans, being sure to cover the adhesive tape. Or paste stretched crepe paper streamers over the entire rattle.

Play it by shaking with vigor or tap it quickly and lightly with your fingers.

CLOTHESPIN CHATTERBOXES

Making clothespin rattles will be fun for everyone and will provide instruments of particular delight for the very young musician. Plan to make at least two clothespin people, a boy and a girl.

Choose clothespins made of one piece of wood. Just below the neck of the clothespin, drill two small holes, one on each side, for arms. Glue one half of a used kitchen match into each hole. Simpler but less satisfactory arms can be made by winding a pipe cleaner around the clothespin neck.

On the top knob of the clothespin, paint or crayon a face. You can make blue eyes and red lips. Paste down a little yarn or two short pieces of rope for the girl's braids or shade in brown or black hair. If you make a mistake in this delicate job, wind adhesive tape around the knob and start again.

You can paint on clothes or paste colorful cloth or crepe paper about the clothespin body. For the girl, use the arms to hold her dress on top and bind her around the middle with a belt of cloth, paper or ribbon. For the boy, wind adhesive tape pants about the legs, or make a belt of tape and convert a skirt into pants by pushing the center portion about the clothespin halves with a pencil point or paper clip. Be sure to paint in shoes across the bottom of the clothespin.

Then make the most important article of clothing, the button hat. Each hat should be a stylish color to go with the rest of the outfit, of course, and each should consist of two bone or wooden buttons. Attach the buttons to the top of the clothespin with a heavy staple or 2 nails long enough to permit the buttons to move about. Drill tiny holes and then hammer the nails in far enough so that they will not come out when you play the rattle.

Play by shaking and by tapping or walking on wood.

BONE RATTLE

The Indians made dance rattles from buffalo and deer claws and hoofs. But the round bones of lamb chops make an effective bone rattle and can be put together with few tools.

You'll need from 4 to 6 of these little bones; each shoulder chop has only one. Clean off the meat thoroughly and dig out the marrow from the center. Soak the bones in hot water and detergent to get rid of all the grease. Then dry them out in the sun.

Usually the bones have a handsome ivory look and need no further decoration. If they are discolored or if you prefer a highly colored rattle, you can paint each bone a different bright color.

With their ready-made center holes, the bones are easy to attach to a ring made from a wire hanger. Unwind the ends of the hanger so that you have a long length of wire. Break off a 10- or 12-inch piece by bending the wire back and forth at the same spot until it snaps. Don't touch the broken ends for a few seconds — they will be hot from the friction. Then thread the bones on.

Wind the ends of the wire around each other, with the help

of pliers if necessary, and make a short handle (see picture). Wrap any sharp points with colorful tape.

Hold the rattle by its taped ends and shake away. Try shaking it slowly side to side for a "change of pace."

You can make the rattle louder by mounting it on a wooden base. Sand down and shellac a slab of scrap wood. Wedge a nail through the two wire bound ends and hammer it to the wood.

PAPIER MACHE MARACAS

Instruments of papier mache are sturdier than those made of paper or cardboard and are fun to make. But don't expect to whip anything up in short order. You need time and patience.

Allow a few minutes before your bedtime one night to start your maracas. Round up half a dozen sheets of old newspaper. Tear the paper into small pieces, and put them into a large pot of hot water to soak until the next evening.

To prepare for the next step, get some laundry starch or make flour paste from flour and *cold* water, cooked for 5 minutes. (Add a few drops of oil of peppermint or wintergreen to prevent the paste from developing a sour odor.)

For this messy operation, better change from street clothes or don an apron. Shred the paper until it is pulp. Do a thorough job of it and then squeeze out the extra water. Add the starch or flour to your paper until the pulp becomes sticky enough to push into shape.

Now crumble one sheet of newspaper into an oval shape (see picture), and tie a string around its bottom so you can mold your instrument around it. Start with a narrow neck, then widen the center portion by applying additional layers of paper. *Don't* make it too thick. When it is shaped like the picture, paste on an outer coat of plain paper, toweling or wrapping paper. Place the maracas in a spot where it can remain 2 or 3 days. It will take that long for the papier mache to dry thoroughly.

Meanwhile prepare your handle. You can use a piece of broomstick or coat hanger or the handle from an old kitchen brush. If you have no scrap wood about, make a handle from doweling (¾ to 1 inch thick) from the hardware store. You can also make a satisfactory handle of papier mache. Use a pencil as the form over which to mold your handle.

When the body has dried thoroughly, ease out the crumbled newspaper and insert buttons or noodles or beans into the maracas. Insert the handle and close up the open spaces around it with adhesive or gummed paper. You can also papier mache it closed.

Paint the body (and handle, if you like) with poster paints or paste on colorful wallpaper. When dry, apply a coat of shellac to body and handle.

Maracas usually are shaken in pairs.

SEASHELL SHAKERS

At the seashore, look for shells — scallop and mussel, and clam and oyster, too. You needn't find the two halves that originally housed the same shellfish. Just find two of nearly the same size and shape.

Fill the shells with pebbles or a bit of sand. If they are small, you can glue them together or run adhesive tape around the edges. Shake them in the palm of your hand.

For the slightly larger shells, make a wooden handle from a good-sized branch or old broomstick. Saw down the center of the handle about 3 inches so that the top of the stick is divided. Thin out the two halves of the stick from the inside with a file and sandpaper so that it looks like this:

With a fine drill, bore two holes toward the top of the wide portion of each shell.

Now sandwich the two halves of shell between the two ends of the sawed handle. Bind handle and shells together with cord or leather lacing.

You might wind a bit of cord around the handle just below the shell so that the wood does not split further.

Shellac shell and handle, or paint on a design.

Hit the handle with a piece of hardwood like a clave.

Or make two shakers and knock their handles together.

COCONUT RATTLES

A coconut can be transformed into an excellent rattle that sounds and looks just right for rhythm — Latin, Hopi or jazz.

Drill a hole at one end of the coconut and let the juice run into a glass. Then bore a good-sized hole (no more than one inch in diameter) on the other end of the coconut. Saw the coconut in half between the two holes you have bored.

Pry the coconut meat out of the shell with a knife until the hard, brown inside is completely exposed. After the coconut shell is thoroughly cleaned, dry it in the sun. Keep the edges of the shell clean as you are going to glue the halves together again.

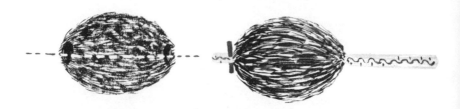

Prepare a handle of one-inch dowel or a section of broom handle at least 12 inches long. Part of it will run through the length of the shell. Whittle the handle down a bit to fit into the smaller hole on top of the shell. Sandpaper it smooth. Then about an inch down from the smaller end (top) of the handle, bore a small hole from side to side.

Put a handful of rice or split peas or dry cereal into the coconut shell. Fit in the handle so that the hole you bored is exposed at the top. Carefully glue the two halves together around the handle. The shell will take the glue well, but let it stand at least overnight.

Make a one-inch peg of a piece of pencil or clothespin or scrap wood. Ease it into the hole you bored through the dowel.

The rattle will have an interesting rustic appearance and you can leave it as is. However, if you prefer, you may shellac the shell or rub it lightly with linseed oil or paint it in bright colors. The handle and peg should be either shellacked or painted.

Of course, don't shake it until glue and paint have thoroughly dried.

GOURD RATTLE

In the world of music, gourds have many uses.

Gourds make fine drums, banjos, and scraping instruments. It was from the gourd that the Indian made his rain rattle. The gourd rattle we'll make is a Latin-American version which has found its way into the music of many composers. It is surprisingly easy to make, too.

Select a large well-shaped gourd, preferably one with a narrow neck handle of its own. Make sure the shell is hard and firm.

Saw off a small section of the narrow neck, but don't throw it away. Pull out the seeds and scrape out the melon meat until the rind is smooth and hard. Dry the rind in the sun and shellac it. Fill the gourd with its own seeds if they sound interesting. Otherwise, use pumpkin or watermelon seeds (or, if necessary, corn, bean, rice, sand or pebbles).

Then either glue the small piece of gourd back on or make a handle to fit in the neck of a length of broomstick or one-inch doweling.

Secure the handle by hammering a heavy nail through the top of the gourd into the top of the wood handle.

String necklaces of pumpkin or watermelon seeds around the outside of the gourd, too.

Shake out those Samba rhythms.

BULL-ROARER

To encourage rain during dry spells, the Indians made rain rattles and thunder music.

They used pine or fir which had been struck by lightning, but you may settle for a scrap of thin soft pine or other light wood. A box slat is fine. Cut out a piece about a foot long and 2 inches wide. Sand the edges. If you like, shape the wood into a feather as the Indians did and paint it red, white and black. Bore a hole toward the top and tie on a long strong string.

Wrap the string around your finger and then twirl your noise-

maker into the air, letting the string unwind as you twirl. You'll hear the roaring of thunder.

Naturally, play this with your drums and rattles.

RATTLES FROM THIS AND THAT

Some of the best sounding rattles can be made from scraps. Look over the ice cream carton, the match box, baking powder can, pepper tin, cleanser container, ink bottle, mayonnaise jar, paper cup. Test them with pebbles or beans or rice or nails.

Try some of these, and then see if you can improve on them.

Shake any of these rattles hard, and you'll get plenty of sound. If you want a drizzle instead of a downpour, move the shakers slowly from side to side.

Shoe Shine Shaker

Shoe polish tins may not bring the rain the Indians made with their rattles, but they add interesting variations of sound to your rhythm band.

Fill one can with a handful or two of dried split peas. Fill the other with uncooked rice kernels. Before you fasten on each top, insert both ends of a 5-inch length of string (thin but strong). When you put on the cover, it will secure the string, giving you a handle.

To make the rattles look as good as they sound, paint them, using the first coat to cover and two more to add a design.

Tennis Ball Racket

With the point of a pair of scissors or of a knife, dig a small hole in an old tennis ball. Force in pebbles and small nails. Close the hole with a patch of adhesive tape. Paint the ball a bright color or sketch in a clown face.

Balloon Babbler

Stuff 3 or 4 paper clips into a balloon. Blow up the balloon and tie it with a rubber band or string. Shake with vigor (you'll be surprised at the *deep* rumble). But stay away from friends with pins.

Bottle Prattle

Soak off the label from an empty ketchup bottle and wash out the inside. Put into the bottle half a dozen nails, screws and bolts, but keep them small or you will break the bottle. Replace the cap. Use the neck of the bottle as a handle, and hold the bottle upside down to shake. The tone will be high and pleasing.

Use tempera paints to decorate the bottle. Try red and black stripes.

Cardboard Maracas

Save the cardboard tube from paper toweling or toilet tissue. Cover one end by pasting on heavy paper or aluminum foil. Fill the tube with dried lima beans. Cover the other end. Finish decorating by wrapping foil about the entire tube or by coloring it with crayon or poster paints.

Tattle Tops

Soda bottle tops make melodic rattles. Remove the cork or cardboard lining, and hammer the cap flat. Then drill or punch a hole through the center of each. To disguise the caps, paint them in different bright colors. Then string them on a length of wire or cord. You can wear this rattler around your arm or neck and shake it by moving while you play another instrument.

Doll Dandy

Ten spools and ten buttons threaded together with elastic or twine make a dandy doll shaker, especially if you add a fancy collar of two bottle caps. With a sharpened nail, punch two holes in the caps. Lay the spools together like this:

Thread through buttons, head, collar and body to one leg. Go back to the head and make the trip again for the other leg. Wind up at the head and tie your two ends together.

Then thread through from one arm to the other, beneath the collar, and then back again the way you came. Tie these two ends together.

Paint or draw in a face and paint or paste on clothes.

The doll will dance a jig and sound the music to go with it.

4. Castanets, Triangles, Cymbals

POP TOP CASTANETS

For dancing fun, soda pop bottle tops make fine castanets.

Each castanet requires a narrow strip of heavy cardboard about 6 inches long, some thin string or yarn and two bottle tops. Plan to make two castanets at a time.

Drill or punch a tiny hole through the center of each of the bottle tops. Then make similar holes one inch from each end of the cardboard.

Place each bottle top, face down, over a cardboard hole. Push string through the holes, with the help of a needle if necessary. Draw the ends of each string together and knot them so that the bottle top is attached tightly.

Center the cardboard in your palm with your thumb and one finger on the bottle caps. When you bring your fingers together, the two caps strike one another and you are ready to tap out a Spanish dance.

To make the castanets more colorful, crayon both sides or paste bits of foil or construction paper on the cardboard.

WALNUT CASTANETS

Castanet comes from a word meaning chestnut, but why not use a walnut for these clappers?

You need two unbroken halves, and so open the shell of the nut carefully. A dull knife inserted in the center will usually do the trick. Remove the nut meat. Drill two holes about half an inch from the edge of each half of the shell. Couple the two sections with colorful string or yarn.

Paint or stain or shellac your castanet, if you like.

Now make another for your left hand.

TRIANGLES

The professional musician's triangle is usually made of a single round length of steel bent to a three-cornered shape with its ends left a short distance apart. It is hung from a gut string and struck with a rod also made of steel.

You can make a satisfactory triangle quite easily however.

Horseshoe Triangle

Visit the local stable or horseback riding school. You'll get a horseshoe for the asking. Suspend the horseshoe from a length of cord or thin wire. Strike it with a large nail.

Coat Hanger Triangle

Go to the coat closet for a selection of wire coat hangers for testing. Hold each by the hook and tap it with a heavy nail. Usually the unpainted hangers sound better than those coated with enamel. You should be able to find one or two musically acceptable triangles.

Brass Tube Triangle

Brass tubing makes an inexpensive, fine-sounding triangle. Use a 12-inch length (about ¼ inch thick) for the triangle and a 6 inch brass rod for the striker. Drill holes through your tube so that you can thread it with a string and hang it up.

Bars

Suspend two steel or iron rods (each about 12 inches long) from a cord or wire so that they hang freely. You will either have to drill holes at one end of each or pound one end to make a lip or saw or file a notch on which to rest the string. Strike across the rods with a striker of the same material or of wood.

CYMBALS

Cymbals are usually hollowed brass plates. These plates can be scraped against one another in a side-swiping motion, or the left cymbal can be held flat and struck by the edge of the right cymbal. For a soft sound, one cymbal is struck with a padded mallet or brush; for great loudness, two drumsticks are used.

Kitchenware Cymbals

Home-made cymbals can be made from pot covers. Test the covers to find one or two of proper ringing tone. Chances are they will be lids of heavy gauge (the thinner aluminum covers have too tinny a sound). If you find one with a bright ring, you can couple it with a less satisfactory pot cover, or strike it with a drumstick. In either case, it will serve your rhythm band well.

Nature Walk Cymbals

Possibly the first cymbals ever used were two stones clashed together. It's a challenge to find stones (possibly slate) to give forth the proper crash.

Makeshift Cymbals

Tin can tops and pie plates can fill in as cymbals. Loosely hammer on handles of dowel or rope loops. The cymbals will be fun to play and almost look like the real thing, but don't expect too much in the way of sound.

Brass Cymbals

You can buy discs of brass to make into cymbals. Through the center of each, drill a hole large enough to thread a bolt and tie on a small leather loop as a handle.

JINGLE CLOGS

Add variety to your percussions with different jingle clogs. They are simple to make.

Cap Tinkles

This instrument has a lovely tambourine-like tinkling. Heavy scrap wood and two soda bottle caps are all you need.

Make the wooden handle 2 inches wide, about 6 inches long and at least ⅝ths of an inch thick. Sand it down, smooth the edges, and shellac or apply a coat of colorful paint.

Prepare your caps by prying out the cork linings from inside (a little hot water helps) and then hammering them flat. Drill or punch a hole through the centers.

Put a nail through the caps into the wood handle at a point about an inch down from the top, but don't hammer the nail so deeply that it prevents the caps from jingling.

Play by holding the jingle clog in one hand and striking it against your other hand.

Tin Clinkers

More jangle than jingle is made by this combination but its tinny music has its own appeal. Scrap wood, two small tin can covers and a nail or screw are the only materials involved.

A frozen juice tin or tomato sauce can is just right. Choose an unopened can. You must drill or punch a center hole in each end, and it is much easier while the covers are on. Make the top hole, then remove the top cover and empty out the food. Make the bottom hole before you remove the bottom cover.

Blunt the edges of your discs with sandpaper or a file.

For your handle, a heavy box slat will do. Cut out a piece 3 inches wide, 6 inches long and at least ⅝ths of an inch thick. You can finish your handle by sanding and shellacking.

Mount your discs loosely on the handle with a long nail or screw. Be sure it allows the discs to move freely.

Shake it and clink away.

Special Clog Handles

To make your jingle clogs look more professional, do a little work on the handle.

Put one of your discs or caps on the wood and draw in a circle that is slightly larger. Sandpaper your wood so that the upper 2 inches of the handle follow the pencilled circle. Whittle down the rest of the stick to form a straight handle about two inches wide. Round out the bottom with sandpaper. Sand down your wood. Then shellac, varnish or paint.

JINGLE RING

Hundreds of years ago, the jingle ring was a much-used instrument.

A wooden or metal embroidery hoop will give you a ready-made frame. If this is not available, you can fashion a hoop by working off the ring around an opened coffee can, or cutting out the center of the coffee can cover. Sandpaper any sharp edges.

You will need 10 to 14 soda bottle caps. Soak the caps and pry out the inside corks. Then hammer along the edges of the tops and flatten them. Drill a hole in the center of each bottle cap.

Attach them in pairs to the hoop with colorful yarn, safety pins, or loops made from wire coat hangers.

You can disguise the ring by winding crepe paper or material scraps around it, or by painting it bright red. If you use safety pins or wire, paint them a contrasting color.

Play the jingle ring by holding it in one hand and striking it with your other hand. Shake it, if you prefer, or put a short stick through the hoop and swing it round and round in a small circle. If you have trouble, grasp the stick with a hand at each end.

JANGLE RING

This is another tin can special. Just combine a metal hoop from the coffee tin or its cover and two tin can tops. (See previous project.)

Punch a hole in the center of each can cover. File down and blunt the edges with sandpaper.

Wind colorful yarn all around the hoop, as in the jingle ring, and leave a 10-inch tail of yarn. Thread this tail through one of the covers, push the cover up about 4 inches and make a knot. Then string on the other can top and secure it with another knot.

Shake or hit it slowly. What kind of bell does it sound like to you?

5. Bells, Chimes and Marimbas

SLEIGH BELLS

Keys strung from a key ring jingle like sleigh bells. The solid one-piece ring is better than the link-type chain, and the larger the keys the louder the bells.

BELL BRACELETS

For a tinkling accent to your drum beats, you can make bell bracelets. Just string on half a dozen tiny bells (the 10-cent store carries them) to colorful yarn, making a knot between each bell. Wrap the yarn around your wrist. When you play the drum, you also shake the bells.

Or put the bracelets on your ankles and stamp when you want bells. Step on one toe and swing your ankle back and forth for a softer tinkle.

BELL STICK

Decorate a 6-inch length of doweling (½ inch to 1 inch in diameter) with colorful paint. When it is dry, staple on a tiny bell or two at each end of the stick. Play by shaking.

TRAIN BELLS

Hang a silver spoon from a wooden rod (use a pencil or a coat hanger). Strike it with another spoon and listen to the coal engine bell. Strike it with wood, and hear the railroad crossing warning bell.

FLOWER POT BELLS

After you've planted the flower outdoors, convert the earthenware flower pot into a bell, but be sure it has no cracks in it. It should have a clear sound.

First, you must get the pot to hang upside down on a string. So that the string won't slip through the pot hole, knot the string and push up to the knot a piece of wood, a tin can cover, or a cork with a hole in the center. Thread the other end of the string through the inside of the pot. Dangle the pot upside down, holding the string in one hand while you strike your bell with a wooden stick or a toy wooden hammer.

If you have more than one flower pot, arrange them to sound from low to high. The larger pots are usually deeper in tone. Suspend them from a wooden rod so that they hang free, and place the rod over the backs of two chairs. Or make a frame by knocking out the top and bottom of a sturdy wooden box. (See picture.) Place the frame on the long side and suspend the pots from what is now the top by looping the string around hooks.

Try tapping out "Ding, Dong, Bell."

STONE BELLS

When you are wandering along the seashore or along country roads, collect a dozen stone bells.

Test them by striking them against one another. You'll want those with a pleasant tone, of course. Stones that have been rubbed smooth and round are easier to handle. Flat stones often make good bells. The Chinese made them of slabs of slate. If you vary the colors, you please the eye as well as the ear.

You will get the best sound out of your bell if you attach heavy cord or a leather thong and hold it by the support. Play by striking it with another stone, with a wooden stick or with a felt-covered hammer.

If your collection is good enough, select three or more bells of different pitch. Suspend them from a rod with the deepest stone on one end and the highest on the other. You can strike out simple tunes.

CHIMES

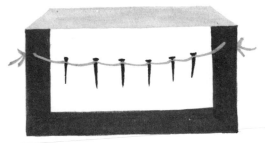

Nail Chimes

Knot large nails or spikes onto a heavy string. Make a frame of a shoebox by removing the bottom and top, laying it on its long side. Attach each end of the string to the frame so that the nails hang down and swing freely. Tap them with another nail.

Brass Rod Chimes

Different lengths of brass rods can be arranged to make sweet-sounding chimes. Drill holes through one end so that you can thread them with string or wire, or saw or file a notch to rest the string on. Place the longest rod on your left and the shortest on the right. Suspend them from a wooden hanger. Or make a frame from a small wooden box.

Tap the pipes with a mallet — a pencil with a spool for a top. For variety, use a ten-penny nail as your striker.

Musical Glasses

Musical glasses so intrigued one of the great musicians of two centuries ago that he toured Europe giving concerts on them. They are easily played and make lovely music.

Fine crystal will sound better but stick to the kitchen variety of glass for your instrument, at least at first.

Start with three glasses. They can be of different shapes and sizes. Line them up according to their tones, if possible. The lowest should be to the left. Sometimes the difference is so slight it cannot be detected. Strike them with a spoon or fork.

Then, with a pitcher of water, make yourself a ladder of sounds by pouring in different quantities of water into each glass. The more water you add the deeper the sound will become.

Test your glasses with the first phrase of "Three Blind Mice." Make the adjustments necessary so that the first word is higher than the second and the second is higher than the third. The higher the number the higher the note.

THREE BLIND MICE

3   2   1

When you have mastered the first three glasses, gradually add five more (4-5-6-7-8) so that you have the full scale. You will be able to finish playing "Three Blind Mice," and add a number of other simple tunes to your repertoire.

Try a stick or pencil to see if you like that sound better than the spoon. You might prefer a stick with a soft felt or cork tip. If you have a tray, you can place the glasses in it, on top of a piece of felt or other soft material so that the glasses can be moved about easily.

Color the water with vegetable dye. You will find it easier to locate the different tones. And, of course, it will look very attractive. Here's the full song to play with the 8 glasses:

THREE BLIND MICE

3 2 1 / 3 2 1 / 5 44 3 / 5 44 3 4/ 8 8 767 85 55
888 767 85 55/ 888 767 855 54 / 3 2 1

MARIMBA OR XYLOPHONE

Once you've made a simple marimba (which is simply a ladder of sound), chances are you'll catch the bug and go on to make bigger and better ones. No scrap of wood will be safe after you've learned the technique of sawing wood into different lengths and hammering out melody. The fun of making this instrument is as great as the pleasure of playing it.

You must learn a few facts before you start.

1. With wood of equal thickness and the same grain, the longer the bar the lower the sound; the shorter the bar, the higher the sound.

   a) To raise the tone of a bar, sand or saw off a little of the bar. Or make the bar thinner by hollowing out the underside slightly with a small plane or spoke-shave.

   b) To lower the tone, make a shallow saw cut across the middle of the bottom.

a   b

2. A bar will not sound if it lies flat on any surface because it is not free to vibrate.

   a) Hold it loosely a quarter of the way from the end of the bar with your thumb and index finger. Tap with a mallet.

   b) Lift the bar from the surface at the place where there is least interference with tone — halfway between the middle and each end.

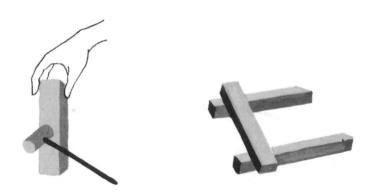

Toybox Marimba

Look to the toy box for a handful of large wooden blocks and a jump rope. Add to these two toy rods (or pencils) and two large wooden beads or empty spools.

Make your two mallets first by fitting a bead or spool tightly onto the end of each rod.

Hold up one of the blocks between the thumb and index finger of your left hand so that it can swing freely. Tap it sharply with one of your mallets. If it gives off a dull thud, put it back into the toy box. Try each block in turn until you get clear-ringing blocks.

You'll find that those twice as wide as they are thick sound best.

From those that sound a note, choose three or more of different lengths and, if possible, of the same width. (A thinner block sounds higher than a thicker block of same length.)

Now fold your rope in the center and lay it on the table or floor in the form of a horseshoe with a narrow opening towards you. The narrow opening should measure half as wide as your shortest block is long. The widest part of the horseshoe should measure half as wide as your longest block is long.

Center the largest block on the wide part of the horseshoe portion so that it overhangs the rope on each side about one quarter of its length. Center the smallest block on the narrowest section so that it overhangs the rope on each side one quarter of its length.

Then fit the other block or blocks over the rope at the point where one quarter of each block laps over.

Now you have a ladder of sound all your own to tap out 3 or 4 note melodies. Have someone accompany you on the drum or rattle.

When you're finished, you can return blocks and rope, rod and bead where they belong.

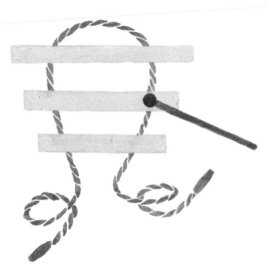

3-Note Marimba

For the toys, substitute a 3-foot strip of wood (one inch x 2 inches) and a length of clothesline or venetian blind cord and make a marimba that you tune to play with other melody instruments.

Prepare your mallet first by gluing a large wooden bead to a 12-inch length of dowel (¼-inch).

Mark the following lengths on your strip of wood:

C — 12 inches
D — 11½ inches
E — 11 inches

Cut your first bar. Hold it loosely between thumb and index finger, and tap it sharply with your mallet. Compare it with C on the piano, pitch-pipe or tuning fork.

Raise the tone if necessary by sanding or sawing. If it is too high, save it for your second or third note.

Saw your second bar and tune it in the same way to D. Finally, tune your third bar to E.

Measure in one quarter of the way from each end of the three bars. Mark the bars on the bottom. Fit your cord over the marks leaving a loop at one end. Attach the cord by hammering in small brads. If you use too large a nail, you will not get a tone.

Hang the marimba on a hook, hold it in your hand or lay it in your lap. Tap out rhythms and simple melodies with one or two mallets.

ONE-OCTAVE MARIMBA

For this larger marimba, get a 7 foot length of pine, basswood, redwood or poplar (1″ x 1⅓″ or 2″), a length of rope, felt or weather stripping and a box of tacks or brads.

Make a wood frame of narrow strips (about ½″ x ½″), like this:

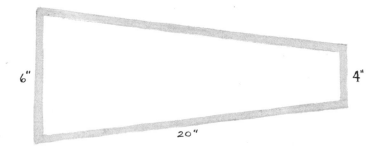

6″   4″

20″

Mark the 8 bars on your long length as follows:

C — 12″	G — 10¼″
D — 11½″	A — 9¾″
E — 11″	B — 9¼″
F — 10¾″	C — 9″

Cut the 12-inch bar first and tune it to C with the help of a piano or tuning fork. Cut each in turn and tune.

When the bars are all tuned, lay them bottom side up half an inch apart. Taper them evenly with the help of rulers.

Center the frame on top of the bars. Draw a line along the outside of the frame. Remove the frame and lay the twine or felt even with the lines you marked. Tack it to each bar.

Lift the nailed bars onto the center of the frame. Tack the ends of the felt to the frame. Add a tack or brads into the frame through the felt between bars 2 and 3 and between bars 6 and 7.

Tap out rhythms and simple melodies with one or two mallets. Put a felt tip on one mallet for a softer sound.

Get together with a friend with a fiber pipe drum, which also has different pitches, for duets.

6. Drums, Drums, Drums

Visit the corner grocer, the hardware store or the garage — or just look at the kitchen shelves again. You can make a drum from almost anything you find.

Your drum need not be round. Drums may be made in many sizes and shapes: square, oval, hour glass, elliptical. Your frame may be of any material from cardboard to crockery. You may attach one drumhead or two, and the drumhead may be made of anything from paper to animal skin.

Here are a few drums, some simple, some more ornate — but each can be put together with little work. Try making some of them, and then use your imagination to invent your own. Always be sure your drumhead is stretched *tight* and attached securely. A section on skin drumheads, which are a little more complicated to attach, begins on page 57.

TIN CAN TOMTOMS

Papoose Tomtom

Replace the cover of a round empty coffee tin with a double layer of wrapping paper glued together and cut into a circle 2 inches larger in diameter than the mouth of the tin. Stretch the paper tight and secure it in place with string or a strong rubber band around the circumference of the tin.

To make the drumhead last longer, cover the paper first with a layer of cheesecloth and then shellac them together.

If you want this miniature tomtom to look interesting, deco-

rate the drumhead and either paint the frame or paste over it with wallpaper or colored paper. It is easier to do this before the drumhead is attached.

To play this tomtom, beat on the top gently with the eraser end of a new pencil or tap it lightly with your fingers.

Squaw Tomtom

For an interesting and an unusually shaped drum, start with the opened tin from a 3- or 5-pound ham as your drum body. Smooth the edges and rough spots with sandpaper.

Cover the body with a thick flat paint, topped with two coats of enamel or paste on decorative wallpaper or decals.

You might throw in a handful of dried lima beans or rice and make this a drum rattle.

Make a drumhead of Patapar, a thin, tough inexpensive paper used in cooking and sold at hardware and department stores. Measure off enough so that there is a good inch or more lap over the edge of your can all around. Then soak the Patapar in water for a few minutes. It will become limp and flexible. Carefully stretch it over your drum body. Bind it by wrapping twine around and around at least 3 times. When the drumhead dries, it will be tight and resonant.

If you have trouble keeping your twine from slipping, make-an "anchor" around the bottom of the tin with another length of twine, lacing from one side to the other, like this:

In playing this drum, try a whisk-broom as a beater for a special "swish" sound.

Brave Drum

Use a large tin can — the giant fruit juice tins are fine — as the body for a drum and two drumheads cut from the old inner tube of a tire.

Soak off the label of the can with hot water. Dry the can and remove *both* ends of the tin with a good can opener. Be sure there are no sharp edges to cut you or your drumheads. Use sandpaper to smooth any rough spots.

A flat paint followed by two coats of quick-drying enamel will disguise the body of the drum. Try an Indian design.

Cut out two circles of rubber 2 inches larger in diameter than your can. Make two garters of thick rubber-band strips of the inner tube. Attach each drumhead by stretching it tightly over the end of the can and looping on the garter to hold it. You will probably need a friend to help you get the proper tautness.

You can also bind the two drumheads by lacing them together. Use thin cord and thread it through a large upholstery or leather-work needle. Just sew from one head to the other making a zigzag pattern.

If you have trouble pushing your needle through the rubber, help it with the point of a knife, but try not to punch a hole.

Make a drumstick from a toy rod and wooden bead. Hit your drumhead with your thumper — as you knock the sides with your knuckles.

Medicine Man Water Drum

An ordinary galvanized or tin pail makes a fine frame for a water drum.

Fill the pail one quarter full of water.

Make a drumhead of a piece of chamois (an old dustcloth will do if you launder it), canvas, khaki, duck, heavy linen, balloon cloth or even oilcloth. Be sure your material is large enough to hang one inch over all sides of the pail. Stretch the cloth tightly over the mouth of the pail and bind it firmly with heavy twine or leather lacing. You can use a hoop of wood or wire to fit tightly around the pail. If your hoop is too large, make it smaller by winding strips of cloth about the entire hoop.

You can give the surface of the drumhead a thin coat of shellac the first or second time you attach it.

Since cloth shrinks when it is wet, you can then make your drumhead tighter by rubbing in water with your hand. Get the drumhead good and wet and swirl around the water in the pail so that it wets the cloth from the inside.

Play the drum while the cloth is wet.

Remove the drumhead after you finish using the drum. Store

drumhead and twine carefully — in the pail if it does not have to go back to more routine duty.

MIXING BOWL DRUM

A wooden chopping, mixing or salad bowl can find a new lease on life with a drumhead of oilcloth or heavy plastic tacked to it.

Drill three holes in the bottom large enough to fit your fingers. These will improve the sound — and enable you to carry the drum. Shellac the bowl or decorate it with paint.

Cut a circle of the oilcloth or plastic about 2 inches larger than the bowl. Center the cloth over the bowl overlapping an equal amount of cloth all around. Hammer in your first tack. Then stretch the cloth across the top of the bowl and place your second tack opposite your first. Place your third tack halfway between the first two, and the fourth opposite the third. Continue to stretch and tack, always first one side and then the other, until you have tacks hammered in every inch or so.

Play your drum with fingers or palms. Or make a beater of a pencil and empty spool.

BASKET DRUM

The Indians used closely woven baskets as drums by placing them on the ground upside down and beating away. Try bread basket, wastepaper basket or laundry basket sizes. Of course, your drum need not be round.

For improved resonance, put the basket right side up and attach a drumhead. Parchment (such as is used for lampshades) would do well for the smaller baskets.

Wet the parchment until it is thoroughly limp. Center it carefully on the basket and tape it to one side of the basket. Then stretch it across the top and tape it on the other side. Holding the parchment taut, wind cord all around the basket.

When the parchment dries, you will have a tight resonant drumhead.

CHEESEBOX HOOP

A round wooden cheesebox cover will supply a hoop, about 2 inches deep, to serve as a frame for a hand drum. Remove the center and sand any rough edges. Use canvas or balloon cloth for your drumhead.

Place your hoop in the middle of the cloth, and fold the cloth over the hoop, using a pin to hold it in place. Then stretch it tightly over the frame, putting in pins every few inches until the entire hoop is covered. Trim off the extra cloth so that the two edges lay flat and a little apart. Then at a point where the cloth covers the hoop smoothly, start sewing with heavy thread from one edge of the cloth to the other. Sew zigzag from one edge to the other. Then start from the other point where the cloth is smooth and sew across the zigzag.

Play this drum while the cloth is wet. Beat with your fingers or make a hard thumper.

Now, go on to skin drums — and cover a cheesebox hoop with goatskin just about as you covered it with canvas. See page 57.

TAMBOURINES

The tambourine with which you can make such gay music is really a shallow drum with loose jingling discs or small bells inserted in its narrow hoop frame. It can be beaten with the bare hand, shaken, or thrown up in the air and caught again. Try Gypsy melodies with the one you make.

Cardboard Bell Tambourine

With half a dozen tiny bells (the 10-cent store carries them), you can make a tambourine that will sound melodic for the time that it lasts.

Use two paper plates — or from laundry shirt cardboard, cut out two circles the size of a dinner plate. (You can trace the outline of a plate.) Place one on top of the other and proceed to pin the bells around the edges with safety pins. Better yet, sew through the two layers of cardboard with heavy cotton or elastic thread and attach 5 or 6 bells loosely on the rim, evenly spaced around the cardboard. Crayon or finger paint a design on the face.

If you have a *round* cereal box top, cut 5 or 6 slits evenly around the edges. Fasten the bells at those places with safety pins or by sewing with elastic thread. Paint or paste over the cover.

Pie Pan Tambourine

With an awl or sharpened nail, punch 6 to 8 holes about the rim of a tin pie pan. Prepare an equal number of 3 inch pieces of thin wire or cord. For each hole you will need two metal discs — bottle tops or metal caps.

Remove any cork or cardboard linings and punch a hole

through each cap. Thread them with the wires and attach them in pairs through the holes in the pie pan. Knot the wires at each end.

Use a coat of flat white paint on the pie pan and then decorate it with enamel.

Cheesebox Hoop Tambourine

You can make a durable, fine-sounding tambourine from the hoop of a round, wooden cheesebox. You'll need some bottle caps and a drumhead of cloth, inner tube or thin calf skin.

Your grocer will supply the cheesebox for the asking. Separate the hoop from the body or cover and sand it down carefully.

Mark on the hoop six rectangles ¾ of an inch deep and about 1½ inches long, an even distance apart around the hoop, like this:

Drill a small hole at a corner of each rectangle to help start your sawing. Then use a coping saw to finish cutting out the rectangles. Drill small holes above and below each rectangle.

Hammer 12 bottle caps flat and drill holes through them. Thread them in pairs on 2 inch lengths of thin wire. Tie one end of each wire to a hole above the rectangle and the other end to the hole below so the caps are loosely centered.

Shellac or paint the hoop.

Attaching the Head

Center your circle of cloth or inner tube so that an equal amount overlaps all around. About half an inch down from the top, hammer in a tack. With the help of a friend, stretch the skin across the top and place the second tack opposite the first one. The third tack should go halfway between the first two and the fourth, opposite the third.

Continue to stretch and tack always working first one side and then the other. You can cover the tacks later with fancy-headed upholsterer's tacks.

DRUMSTICKS OF SORTS

Like the drums themselves, drumsticks can be whipped together from items in the toy box, the sewing kit, the family desk. For less makeshift sticks, the hardware store and the nature walk may supply the necessary wood.

A little imagination will enable you to make the perfect beater for your drum. Try several before you settle on a particular type. Band and orchestra drummers use more than one kind of stick on the same drum to vary the sound.

Drumsticks can differ in size and shape, but the most important difference is the degree of hardness. A hard beater is one with a knob or tip of wood, and it makes the louder sounds.

A beater is softened by wrapping it with leather, felt, sponge, rubber, cork, feathers, lamb's wool or other materials, but the smaller drums cannot be struck effectively by a drumstick which is padded.

Remember, a drum can often be played most interestingly by thumping with hands or tapping with fingers. Try scratching the drumhead with your fingernails while knocking it on the sides with your knuckles.

Here are some suggestions for your beaters. See what you can do with the materials you have available.

PENCIL STICK

Make drumsticks for your smaller drums of unsharpened pencils with eraser tops. Sandpaper the wood end smooth and round. Tap gently with either end.

BEAD BEATER

Glue a large wooden bead (round, oblong or flat) to the end of a pencil, toy rod or small paint brush handle. Cover the bead and the stick with a coat of bright paint, and you won't know they were ever apart.

BALL BEATER

For a softer thumper, attach a tiny rubber jack ball to a rod. With a knife point, punch a small hole and glue the ball to your rod with rubber cement.

SHOETREE THUMPER

A shoe tree makes a fine flexible drumstick. Use the toe end as a handle and tap with the small heel knob.

TURKEY DRUMSTICK

Take the large drumstick from the turkey and put it into service. Wash it thoroughly, sand off any rough spots and dry it in the sun. Handle it gently or it will split.

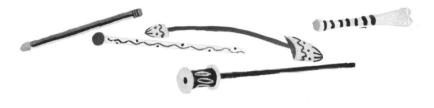

WHISK BROOM BRUSH

To add the soft touch of the wire drum brushes, rub your drumhead with a whisk broom.

DOWEL DRUMSTICK

To make drumsticks of just the right size, buy a length of ⅜th-inch doweling from the hardware store. Each stick should be from 15 to 18 inches long.

You can make a simple stick by just rounding off the ends.

Or sandpaper one end slightly and fit on a small spool as a knob. Put in a dot of glue so that they will not come apart while you are playing. Shellac the doweling and the knob or paint them both.

You may paste on the knob a thin cushion tip of felt, cork or adhesive tape.

PAPIER-MACHE KNOB

A good hard beater can be made with a papier-mache knob. Saw a circular groove near the top of a length of doweling or branch to prevent the papier-mache from slipping off.

Crumple a 3-inch square of newspaper to serve as your base. Wrap it around the stick above the groove. Tear 2 or 3 sheets of newspaper into ½-inch strips (2 or 3 inches long). Prepare a jar of loose flour-and-water paste. Dip the ½-inch strips (one at a time) into the paste and press them onto the crumpled newspaper and to the groove of the stick. Paste until the entire base is covered. Then add more layers of paste-wet papier-mache until your knob is about an inch wide.

Paint or crayon the beater, if you like, and shellac.

TREE THUMPER

Any stick from 10 to 20 inches long will do as a drumstick, but if you have your choice of a raw wood, select a section of hardwood sapling — white oak, hickory, ironwood, ash or elm. It should be about ½ inch thick. If your sapling is an inch or more in diameter, split it lengthwise.

Remove the bark. Whittle or file the stick to a thickness of about ⅜ths of an inch in the center and ½ inch at the ends so that it will spring as you beat with it.

You can finish the playing end of your stick by merely rounding it off slightly. Or you may fashion a little knob at the end by leaving the stick thick there and sandpapering it round.

You can also make the knob by whittling the end of the stick until it is stringy and then submerging the stringy portion in water and tying it back into a knot. File and sandpaper the knot into a knob with no sharp edges to cut the drum.

CURVED THUMPER

At one end of a 20-inch stick, whittle a length of about 6 to 8 inches until it is stringy. Soak it in water and then bend the stringy section into a 3-inch circle on one side of the stick. Lash the end to the stick with string or twine.

This is a particularly good beater for an earthenware or water drum.

SOFTENED THUMPER

To soften a stick or dowel without a knob, cut a strip of scrap wool (perhaps an old blanket) one inch wide and about 2 feet long. Coat the first 6 inches of the wool with glue and wrap it around the end of the stick. When this dries, it will make a hard core. Do not glue the rest of the wool strip, but continue wrapping until you have a roll one inch wide and one inch thick around the end of the stick. Cut off the rest of the material.

With a needle and heavy thread, sew through the end of the material all around and up and down to make it stay securely in place. You may cover the roll with a piece of canvas or chamois cloth and tie it tightly with cord around the shank of the stick.

Fiber pipe drum set (see page 67).

7. Skin Drums

SKIN DRUMHEADS

Once you've learned how to put on a drumhead tightly, why not make the real thing? A drum is one musical instrument you need never buy. You can make a drum to compare with a more expensive store-bought drum and have the fun of creating the instrument yourself.

Best results are obtained with rawhide — untanned skin before it is turned into leather with oak bark or other tannin. Tanned hide does not shrink and tighten when it dries as rawhide does and therefore is better reserved for water drums.

Throughout the world, drums are made with the skin of animals native to the area — tigers, elephants, antelopes, zebras, monkeys or deer. Goatskin and calfskin (and possibly sheepskin) are the best available materials for us.

Animal skins for drumheads can be bought from music stores, music mail order houses or hobby shops. Many instrument stores have old drumheads in their repair shop, and these will not be as expensive as new ones. New skins, depending on their size, cost from 50 cents up. Order a skin 3 or 4 inches larger in diameter than your frame.

If you buy a whole skin, cut it to size with sharp shears while it is dry.

Always soak your skin in cold water until it is flexible enough to attach — at least 30 minutes.

Skins can be attached to frames in many ways, depending on the frame. You can tack, lace or tape, bind with cord or thong or force a hoop of wood or metal over the top.

Never play your drum until the skin has dried overnight.

Make some of the drums described in detail here. Then put your imagination to use and invent your own.

BARREL CONGA

A few readily available materials combine with a goatskin drumhead to make a handsome, durable drum. This drum produces a fine resonant sound and the cord and bead system of attaching the head provides for its periodic tightening so that the drum always sounds as good as new.

Materials

The body should be a nail keg or small barrel. Ask your hardware store to save one for you. You will also need a long length of old venetian blind cord or light clothesline and 7 or 8 wooden beads with holes at least ⅜ths of an inch in diameter. If you have metal tubing, cut one inch pieces as substitutes for the beads.

For the hoop you need, you may be lucky enough to find a fruit basket with a wooden hoop 2 inches larger in diameter than your barrel. Otherwise, perhaps you can get the local garage or welder to bend a ¼ inch metal rod to a circle of the proper size and weld it together. A good substitute hoop that you can prepare yourself is made of wire — coat hanger wire will do. Twist the ends together, file them smooth and bind the joint with tape so that the edges can't cut through the skin.

From the music store or drumhead supply company, buy a goatskin head about 4 inches larger than the diameter of the barrel.

Preparing the Barrel

Remove the ends of the barrel, leaving it open top and bottom.

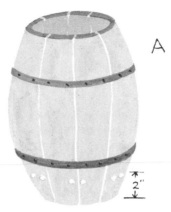

A

2"

File the edges very smooth and put adhesive tape over any sharp edges of the rim to avoid tearing your drumhead.

Strengthen the metal rims by drilling and bolting them with small bolts and nuts or wood screws to the wooden barrel so that they won't slip after the drum has been used for a time.

Draw a line around the barrel 2 inches from the bottom. On this line, drill two ¼ inch holes about ¾ of an inch apart. (See picture A.) Mark and drill 7 more pairs of holes evenly spaced along the line you drew around the drum. Smooth the edges of the hole with sandpaper or countersink.

You may sand the barrel and varnish or paint it. If you paint it, use a flat white paint as a base and decorate or overcoat with colorful enamel.

Preparing the Skin Drumhead

Center the hoop on the skin and draw a line on the skin with a pencil around the outside edge of the hoop.

Then soak the skin in COLD water at least half an hour. It will not do the skin any harm to remain in water longer.

When the skin is soft, squeeze out excess water and lay the skin flat on your work table. Lay the hoop along the pencilled line and begin to tuck the outer edge of the skin around the hoop

B

C

and underneath. Be sure to keep the hoop in line with the pencilled circle. As you tuck, take a large needle and heavy thread and sew the skin to the hoop wrapping the thread around the hoop so that the skin is firmly attached to it. (See picture B.) It may not appear too tight when the skin is wet, but when it dries, it will tighten around the hoop and become very firmly attached. Keep adding water to the skin, sprinkling it on, or lay a wet sponge in the middle of the skin to keep it wet while you sew.

Just inside or next to the hemmed rim of the skin, punch 8 holes, evenly spaced around the edge. Use a punch awl or a large nail with a sharpened point. The holes are for the rope to pass through.

Readying the Beads

Prepare your beads by countersinking or filing the holes slightly to widen the top and to prevent rubbing against the rope. If you have metal tubes, flare the ends slightly with a flaring tool or child's wooden top tapped into the hole to spread it slightly. Smooth the edges. (See picture C.)

Attaching the Head

Get ready to thread the drumhead to the body. Take up your cord or line. Tie a knot about 4 or 5 inches in from one end for a tail. You will later attach the other end of the cord to the tail as you come around the other side of the drum.

With the knot on the inside of the barrel, pass the rope through the right-hand hole of one of the pairs. (See picture D.) Thread a bead onto the rope.

Stand the drum upright and place the drumhead on top with

the hemmed part of the hoop next to the barrel so that you cannot see the tucking from the outside. (See picture E.)

Then pass the rope up over the outside edge of the barrel through a hole in the skin and down through another bead. Continue downward to the first left-hand hole of the next pair of holes to the *right*. Thread the rope through the left-hand hole, and back again out through the right-hand hole and up through the second bead.

Continue in this manner around the drum, being sure to leave the rope loose until you have it completely threaded around the drum. You will come back to your first bead and down to the first left-hand hole to tie the rope to the tail inside. Make a knot once your cord is inside the barrel, but do not join the two ends until the cord is tightened.

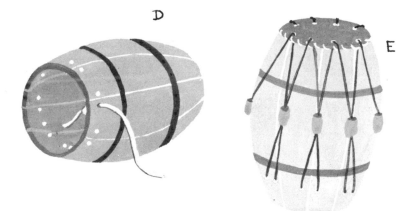

D

E

Tightening the Cord

Keep the beads at the bottom of the drum. Then press down firmly on the rim of the drumhead (you might get someone to help you do this) and begin to tighten the rope. Try to keep the head fairly level by not pulling too hard on one side at a time. Thread the slack rope until it is all centered at the point where the ends of the rope are knotted. Tie them together. (See picture on page 81.)

Handle

If you have a great deal of rope left after tightening, you can make a braid handle. Drill a hole through the middle of the barrel, and loosely pass the rope through it and back to the bottom holes. Secure the extra length to the rope there and cut off the rest of the cord. Cut 3 lengths about equal to the extra piece. Knot the 3 lengths together about half an inch from one end, and braid them together by alternately crossing the left and the right ropes over the center rope. Stop braiding half an inch from the end and make another knot. Tie the braid handle to the extra length of rope attached to the barrel.

Finishing the Drum

Allow the drumhead to dry overnight. *Don't* strike it at any time while it is still wet. Then push the beads up as far as they will go. Your drum will be as tight as it can be.

Beat it with your palms or with a soft or medium-hard drumstick. You get the best tone by beating off center, near the edges of the drumhead, instead of right in the middle.

COCONUT DRUMS

When coconuts find their way to your local market, look for one or two with which to make coconut drums. Made with a skin drumhead, the coconut drum is an asset to a band and a handy size for marching or for dancing.

Tap the coconut with your knuckles and listen for a hollow sound. Select one with no cracks in the shell. Your drumhead should be of goat or lamb skin about 4 inches wider in diameter than the coconut. Since you will need such a small skin, perhaps the music store will have a second-hand drumhead from which you can salvage enough for your drumhead.

The only other materials you will need will be a ball of heavy twine and a wire coat hanger.

Preparing the Coconut Body

Decide which section you want to use for your drum. Drill a hole in the waste end to let the juice run out. Be sure to catch it in a glass or small pitcher — it's very tasty.

Draw a line around the coconut about 1½ inches from the top. Use a sharp saw and cut through the coconut. Starting it will be a little hard but once a cut is begun, it will go quickly and easily.

Pry the coconut meat out of the shell with a knife until the hard, brown inside is completely exposed. Then use a sharp knife or chisel to peel off the loose shreds from the outside shell. Sand it smooth, and with a file or sandpaper, smooth the sawed rim.

Decorating the Shell

You may shellac the coconut shell or rub it lightly with linseed oil. After it is thoroughly dry, rub it smooth with steel wool.

Otherwise, paint it with bright colors using an Indian or African design.

Preparing the Skin

Soak the skin in COLD water for at least half an hour.

Measure around the mouth of the coconut, and then cut off a length of twine about 6 inches longer. Tie the two ends of the twine together.

When the skin is soft, squeeze out some of the water and lay it flat on the table. Start tucking the outer edge of the skin around the circle of twine. With a large needle and heavy thread, sew the skin to the twine wrapping the thread around so that the skin is firmly attached.

While the drumhead is still wet (sprinkle it with water if necessary), take a large nail with a sharpened point or a punch awl and punch holes in the drumhead, about an inch apart, just inside the hem. The holes should be just large enough for the twine to pass through.

Making the Ring

From a light gauge wire or thin coat hanger, make a ring 2 to 2½ inches wide. You'll need a length of wire from 6 to 8 inches long. Use wire-cutting pliers or tin snips to cut off excess wire. Join the two ends of the wire, twist them together with the pliers and fit the ring over the bottom of the coconut shell.

Attaching the Head

Place the skinhead on top of the coconut shell with the hem face down. Continue to keep the skin wet by sprinkling it or dabbing it regularly with a sponge.

Unwind your ball of twine. You will need a length from 10 to 12 feet. Fold the twine at the center and pass the twine to the center fold under the ring about the bottom of the coconut shell. Then, without pulling, bring one end of the twine up over the shell, over the rim of the skin and down through the punched hole and then back again under the rim. Leave the twine fairly loose and string it around the coconut until you have used up the string. Do the same thing with the other end of twine.

When the twine is strung entirely around the coconut, begin to tighten the twine, not too much the first time. Once the head stays in place, grip the edge of the hem of the skin with pliers and pull the skin down. Work the twine to the ends and tie them together.

Finishing the Drum

Allow the skin to dry overnight. *Don't* play your drum until the skin is thoroughly dry.

Use fingers and palm to play. Or make a small drumstick of thin wood.

VARIABLE PITCH COCONUT DRUM

To make the coconut a drum with a variety of pitches, make a triangular hole in the bottom of the shell.

With a ¼-inch drill, drill out three holes in the bottom of the coconut, about 1½ inches apart, like this:

Then use a coping saw to cut out the bottom piece between the holes, like this:

File or sandpaper the edges smooth.

Handle

After the drumhead is attached, tie both ends of a short length of heavy cord to the side cords, making a loop large enough to fit snugly around your middle three fingers.

Playing

Grip the shell with your thumb and little finger, and fit your middle three fingers through the loop. Press your palm against the hole, opening and closing it as you tap the drum with the fingers of your other hand. You may get as many as five different tones.

COCONUT BONGOS

You can make a pair of coconut bongos by fitting two prepared coconut shells with a joining piece of wood shaped to the curve of the shells.

Make a paper pattern with a sheet 3 inches long and 2 inches wide. Place one of the 2-inch sides of paper 1½ inches down from the top of one of the coconut shells. With scissors, cut the paper to fit the contours of the shell. Mark this side and its shell "A." Then do the same on the other 2-inch side with the other shell, marking them "B."

Set the shells upside down on a table and fit the paper pattern between them so that they join. Trim the paper so that the 3-inch sides are parallel to the table.

Now lay the pattern on a piece of wood (2 inches thick) and trace the outlines on the wood. Label sides "A" and "B." With coping, hack or keyhole saw, cut the wood along the lines.

About half an inch from the top, draw a line joining sides "A" and "B." Do the same thing half of an inch from the bottom.

Anchor your wood in a vise. With a sharp drill, drill a hole straight through the length of the 3-inch piece. Then readjust the wood in the vise and drill the second hole through. The holes should be large enough to fit a 3-inch stove bolt.

Fit the wood to shell "A" and mark the position of the top hole with a long nail or punch awl. Drill your hole.

Slip the 3-inch stove bolt through the hole in the shell and the top hole of the wood. Mark the position of the bottom hole with an awl. Remove the bolt and drill.

Repeat the procedure for shell "B."

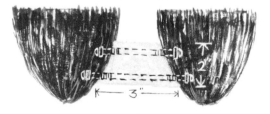

If you haven't sawed an accurate contour in the wood, use a scrap of felt (from an old hat, perhaps) and cut a piece to fit between the shell and the wood joiner at each end. This will allow you to tighten the bolts firmly without danger of cracking the shell. If you have enough felt, put a piece on the inside of each shell, too — it will not affect the tone.

Stain, varnish, shellac or paint the wood.

Attach the skin drumheads the same way as for the lone coconut drum.

FIBER PIPE DRUM SET

The skillful drummer or band of drummers will want to make a set of fiber pipe drums of different pitch. Heavy tacks easily transform the alien fiber pipe into a ready ally of a skin drumhead. The results are exciting.

The Body

Fiber waste pipe is used normally in rural areas for drainage of waste to cesspools away from the house or barn. Any country builder or large mail order house will sell you fiber pipe at about 40 cents a foot. The pipe runs about 4 inches in diameter and comes in 7 or 8-foot lengths, enough to provide you with 7 drums.

The longer the pipe, the lower will be the pitch, but 26 inches is the longest pipe advisable for a good sound.

With an ordinary hand saw, cut your 96 inches into 7 drums: 8 inches, 10 inches, 12 inches, 14 inches, 16 inches, 20 inches and 26 inches.

File or sandpaper the saw cuts smooth but not round. The skin sounds better over an edge.

Preparing for the Tacks

You may use heavy carpet tacks or hammered brass upholstery tacks to attach the drumhead to the body. Carpet tacks (#14 size) are cheaper, but brass tacks are more attractive.

Drill small holes for the tacks instead of forcing them directly into the fiber to prevent the tacks from bending. For the #14 carpet tack, use a small drill; the 1/16th inch drill is fine. For the hammered brass tacks, which have an even smaller shank, you will need a very small gauge drill, number 61 to 65, and you will have to hammer in the tacks carefully.

To lay out the marks for the holes, use a 16 inch piece of masking or adhesive tape. Make a pencil or crayon mark on the tape every ⅝ths of an inch. Then place the tape around the drum about ½ to ¾ of an inch below the top. (It is better to make it ¾ of an inch unless your drumhead is less than 7 inches in diameter.) (See picture A.)

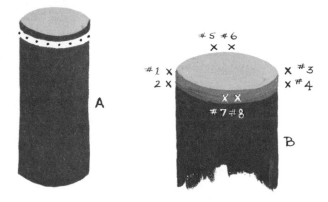

Drill a hole at each of the marks. Don't worry about the drill getting gummed with tar. It will drill perfectly well, and you can clean it later with benzine, gasoline or lighter fluid.

It will make your tacking even easier if you now take a larger drill, about ⅜ths of an inch, and countersink holes the slightest bit — just enough to make a slight hollow so that you can locate the hole by feel instead of having to lift up the skin each time to see where the hole is. Don't countersink much or your tacks may not hold well.

The Drumhead

For each drum you will need a sheep or goat skin about 8 inches in diameter. Try to work out a special purchase from your music store or drumhead mail order house.

Soak each skin at least half an hour in COLD water until it is soft. However, the skin must remain wet while you work on it, and so it is advisable to leave it in the water until you are ready for it.

Attaching the Head

The process for attaching the skinhead to each drum is the same, whatever its size. You will need the help of another person.

When your skin is soft and wet, center it over an open end of pipe so that an equal amount of skin overlaps all around it. Near the bottom of the overlap, feel around for one of the holes you drilled and hammer in your first tack. Put your second tack in the hole ⅝ths of an inch away. Then stretch the skin across the top of the pipe. Let your helper grip it tightly with pliers while you hammer the next pair of tacks into holes opposite the first pair. The third set of tacks should go halfway between the first two, and the fourth pair should go opposite the third. (See picture B.) Before each pair is hammered, stretch the skin with pliers and pull very tightly.

Continue to stretch and tack the skin always working first one side and then the other. DON'T put the tacks all on one side at a time or you will have a lopsided drumhead.

Tuning the Drums

The longest pipe will have the deepest sound, and the shortest pipe will have the highest sound. With 7 drums (of different sizes) you can arrange a ladder of 7 different notes. But if you want to tune the drums to definite sounds to compare with piano notes, for instance, you will have to further tune them with the drumhead attached. The tightness of the skin also determines the pitch.

Select the finished drum of the set you have made which is closest in sound, though a little low, to the pitch you want.

Use either of the following methods:

1) Turn the drum upside down and start sawing off pipe a little at a time until you have the required pitch.

2) With a one-inch bit, drill holes in a line on the side of the drum until you reach the desired pitch. Get some corks, about an inch wide, so that if a hole is drilled too high, you can cover it. (See picture C.)

Playing the Drums

Play these first with the ends of your fingers. Slap them near the outside rim of the drumhead. (See picture on page 56.)

STOVE PIPE DRUM

You can easily make a sturdy drum from a scrap of stove or drain pipe, and a long length of the thin metal pipe can be cut into varying sizes for a set of different pitches.

Each drum requires a skin drumhead (4 inches wider in diameter than the pipe), coat hanger wire or similarly heavy wire and a ball of heavy twine.

The pipe itself may measure from 8 inches to about 26 inches.

Preparing the Pipe Body

File or sandpaper the top edge of the pipe so that it is smooth but not blunted.

About 6 to 8 inches below the top of the pipe, draw a circle all around the pipe. Drill two ⅛th-inch holes on the circle half an inch apart. Measure off an inch, and make another pair of holes half an inch apart. Continue to make pairs of holes every inch until you have a row of holes completely around the pipe. (See picture A.)

Thread your wire in and out of the holes so that the longer length of wire is on the outside of the pipe. (See picture B.) Fasten the wire together inside the pipe, using a pliers to bind the ends. Don't make the wire too tight. You will be slipping cord underneath it to anchor on the drumhead.

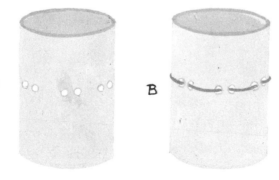

A   B

Short Pipe Drum

If you plan to use a very short length of pipe from your drum, it would be wise to discard the wire-and-cord system of attaching the skin. *Don't* drill the holes in the pipe.

Instead, cut out very narrow wedges at the bottom of the pipe. (See picture C.)

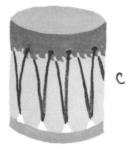

C

Fasten short pieces of tape at the top of each wedge to prevent the metal from cutting through the cord. Bind all around the bottom of the pipe with tape to prevent the edges from being pulled in when you tighten the head.

Preparing the Skin Drumhead

Make a twine hoop for your drumhead. Find its required size by encircling the outside of your pipe with twine and adding about 6 inches to this measurement. Cut off this length of twine; knot the ends together.

Stretch the twine hoop into the form of a circle in the center of the skinhead. With a pencil or black crayon, draw the circle onto the skin by tracing around the outside of the twine.

Then, soak the skin in COLD water at least half an hour.

When the skin is soft, squeeze it out a little and lay it flat on the table. Put your twine hoop on the penciled circle. Start winding the skin about the twine, tucking it under. Sew around the hoop with heavy thread. Tuck and sew until the skin is hemmed about the entire hoop.

While the drumhead is still wet (sprinkle it with water if necessary), take an awl or a large nail with a sharpened point and punch holes an inch apart just inside the hem. The holes should run in a row all around the drumhead. (See pictures on page 60.)

Attaching the Drumhead

Fold your twine at the middle and slip it through the wire (or about the wedge) until the fold. Start lacing through the holes and back to the wire or wedge, leaving the twine fairly loose, until you are halfway around the pipe. Then go back to the fold and lace the other way. When the two ends of the twine meet, start tightening the twine.

Keep the skin wet while you tighten by constantly dabbing it with a sponge. Tighten as evenly as possible and work the loose twine around to the ends. Then tighten again, pulling the twine with pliers. Tie the two ends together tightly inside the pipe.

Finishing the Drum

Allow your drum to dry overnight. *Don't* play it until it is thoroughly dry.

Set of Drums

Make any number from 3 to 7 drums ranging from 8 to 26 inches in length. The longest pipe will have the deepest sound.

For tuning drums, see fiber pipes, page 70.

DRUM SET FRAME

To improve the tone of your drums lift the open ends off the table or floor by suspending them from a frame.

Making the Hooks

Make hooks from coat hanger wires. Reshape each wire to form an "S" so that the top of the hook can rest on the top edge of the frame and the bottom of the hook can curve under the lower lip of the drum. Tie a piece of cord tightly around the drum and "S" hook binding the hook to the drum shell to keep the drum from falling off. (See picture A.)

Vary the length of the hooks by fitting them to the length of the drums so that the drumheads will all be at the same level. They are easier to play in this position.

Chair Rack

Hang 3 or 4 drums on the back of a low-backed wooden chair, sit backwards on the chair, and you are set to play.

Barrel Rack

Use a large, light barrel of fiber or wood — the kind moving and storage companies use. Hang your drums from the top rim, both inside and outside the barrel. (See picture B.)

Square Frame

Use a sturdy, deep box and place it so that the open end is up. Hang your drums from the side of the box with the longest drum to the left. Arrange the drums in order of size so that the shortest is at the extreme right.

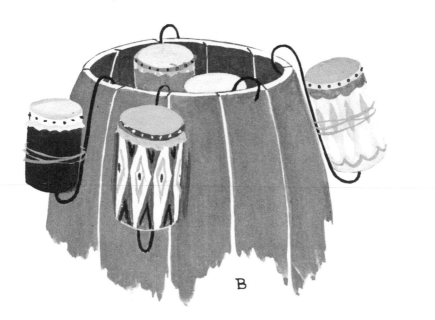

B

8. Odds and Ends for Rhythm Bands

You've now been able to make enough instruments to start a rhythm band. In this chapter are some more rhythm instruments, some you can make in a hurry out of available odds and ends when an extra friend shows up in the middle of a session. Some of these emergency instruments can be saved for the next get-together.

SALT BOX DRUM

A barrel-type salt box makes a good last-minute drum even if the box is not quite empty. Just tap the top with the rubber end of a pencil. Pound the box against the table with your left hand and the salt inside adds a rattle.

You can make the drum sturdier by pasting a double layer of wrapping paper on the top. Decorate and shellac if you wish.

BAND BOX DRUM

A hat box which already has holes punched for a handle converts easily into a makeshift parade drum. Just lengthen the handle string, and keep the top tight.

SCRAPING SCREW

Run a nail over the turns of the longest screw you can find in the tool box. You will make the sound louder by resting the top end of the screw on an overturned bowl or opened tin can. Vary the sounds by tapping the screw itself on the bowl or can.

TEN-PENNY TRIANGLE

Knot a string around the neck of the largest nail available. It should be at least 3 inches long and will sound better if 5 inches long. Hold the string in the air with one hand and strike the large nail gently with a medium-sized nail or brad. It will tinkle like a triangle.

When you have time to visit the hardware store, pick up a few giant spikes.

PAPER BAG MARACAS

Put bottle tops, beans, pebbles or even marbles into a small paper bag or sack. Blow up the bag and encircle the opening with your fingers so that the air will not escape. Then tie the bag with stout string or a rubber band. Shake away.

You can decorate the bag with poster paint, crayon or chalk. A coat of shellac will make it stronger.

BRAD BELLS

Cup a handful of tiny nails or brads in your hand and jingle away. They make fine tiny bells.

STRING BASS

A clothesline or old venetian blind cord makes wonderful bass fiddle rhythm if you have a length of 4 feet or more. Attach one end to a door knob or waist-high heavy piece of furniture. Stretch the other end tightly to a wooden floor and keep a foot on it firmly. Pluck away in time to the music.

KETTLE DRUM

A metal tray will serve as a kettle drum. Make a beater from a length of broom handle softened by an old wool sock tied on with a rubber band or string.

COAT BUTTON CASTANETS

String 3 or 4 coat buttons loosely on yarn or string, and knot the ends of the yarn. Wind the yarn around one hand, placing the buttons in your palm. Move the buttons by opening and shutting your fingers.

Try making castanets from different types of buttons. Wooden buttons are best, but bone and brass buttons provide variety of pitch. Avoid buttons covered with material.

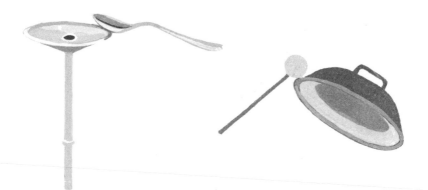

BASKET STEM BELL

The stem from the coffee percolator basket can be put to good musical use. Make the stem the handle, and strike the bottom with a spoon or pencil. The sound is more bell-like if you hold the stem upside down when you play it.

BUTTON ANKLE RATTLES

Just string a length of yarn or ribbon with a dozen or more buttons made of plastic or bone. Avoid using buttons covered with material and save the brass buttons for other jobs.

Make a knot on each end of the yarn so that the buttons will not slip off. Then tie the ends together around your ankle with a bow or double knot. Hop and stamp in rhythm.

POT COVER GONG

The lid of a heavy cast iron pot will stand in as a gong. Hold the pot cover by its handle and strike the edges of the cover gently with a stick padded with absorbent cotton. Also swish your lid with a scrub brush.

HOT TIN CAN

Run an empty tin can in rhythm over the ridges of an exposed steam radiator. Make the same trip with a wooden block.

TRIANGLE FORKS

Suspend a fork from a string and strike it with another fork. The delicate sound will do fine for the extra triangle you need.

TEMPORARY TAMBOURINE

Shake three coins (nickles or quarters) in your hand in time to the music. You get the likeness of a tambourine.

WHISK BROOM SWISH

Brush the wooden table or floor with a whisk broom, but put your mind on the rhythm instead of the dirt.

SPOON SYNCOPATORS

For rhythm with a metallic accent, hold two teaspoons lightly by their handles and crash the backs of the teaspoon bowls together.

With a little practice, you can handle the spoons as though they were castanets and perhaps play a pair in each hand. Hold one spoon between your middle and index fingers and the other between your index finger and thumb.

WOODEN SPOON RHYTHM

From cake baking to music making is an easy switch for wooden mixing spoons. Knock them together like rhythm sticks. Then beat them on the metal wastepaper basket, the wooden floor or the leather chair.

Percussion band with melody played by flower pot bells (page 35), marimba (page 39), and fiber pipe drums (page 67). Other instruments shown include barrel congas (page 58), coconut drum (page 62), minstrel bones (page 10) and shakers (page 16).

9. Strings

TUBER HARP

Take a rubber band of any thickness from the family desk and you are ready to make your harp.

Bite down on one end of the rubber band and loop the other end around your left index and middle fingers. Pluck gently with your right hand. The more you stretch the band, the higher will be the tone, so you can play a simple melody by moving your left hand to and fro. But don't stretch the band too much or your efforts at music will be repaid by a broken instrument and a stinging face.

Try out rubber bands of different sizes and widths (thicker bands sound deeper). Practice a little and you may even get someone to recognize the tune you are playing.

WISHBONE HARP

Save that wishbone from the dinner chicken or turkey for a tiny wishbone harp. String a small thin rubber band across the opening. Wind the band over several times if necessary.

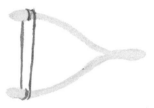

You won't get much sound if you pluck in the air. Rest the open end of your wishbone on a piece of wood or empty can and pluck it gently. It should be fun to see how much melody you can coax from your miniature instrument.

SLINGSHOT STRUMMER

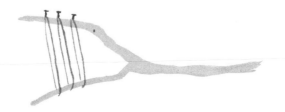

In the park or in the woods, look for a Y-shaped branch to make a strummer.

Put in three screws to use as pegs along one prong and stretch on three rubber bands. Use bands of the same size and scale your strings by stretching them so that each one is tighter than the one below it.

URBAN SLINGSHOT STRUMMER

If you cannot easily find a forked branch, make a frame for a rubber band strummer.

Join two 12-inch sticks with a 4-inch cross piece at the bottom and a 2-inch cross piece at the top. String on as many as 8 rubber ba ds. Keep all the bands the same size. Those toward the bottom will be stretched more and therefore sound higher.

SHOEBOX STRUMMER

A cardboard cigar or shoe box supplies a ready-made frame. Remove the cover and use only the open box.

Half an inch from both ends of the shorter sides, cut small grooves with an ordinary kitchen knife. Place your box so that the longer sides face you. Select your thinnest, shortest rubber band. String it around the box and fit it into the pair of grooves nearest you. Then into the grooves on the far side, put your widest, longest band.

Measure off 2 more pairs of grooves an equal distance between the 2 end grooves. String on 2 more rubber bands grading them as to size.

Pluck the strummer with your fingers or a used kitchen match stick.

BOX BANJO

Raid the kitchen for the main ingredient for a box banjo. It can be cooked up in a matter of minutes but it sounds surprisingly like the real instrument.

Search for a sturdy small carton — from cereal or dry milk or whipped butter, for instance. It may be square or round but should not be more than 2 inches deep. Use scotch tape or gummed paper to anchor the cover on or to seal the spout.

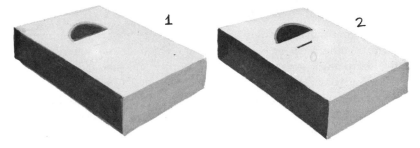

Lay the box flat on its widest surface and carve away. One inch from the left edge, cut out a semi-circular sound hole. (See picture 1.) Another inch down to the right, cut a 1-inch slit (Picture 2).

To make a bridge, cut a 2-inch square of heavy cardboard. From two corners remove half an inch squares. Your bridge will have a one-inch tab (Picture 3).

Fit the bridge into the slit, and string your banjo with 4 rubber bands of different sizes. The smaller ones will stretch more and play higher notes. Pluck them gently with your fingers or with a used kitchen match.

WIRE HANGER HARP

With a shoelace, a box and a handful of hangers you can make an intriguing harp on which to pluck rhythms and sound effects. The harp music goes nicely with a recorder and subdued drum, too.

Your box may be a sturdy cigar box or a wooden candy box. The lace can be a long shoelace, heavy twine, a good-sized leather boot lace or a strip of leather. You will also need 3 or 4 wire coat hangers and about 6 inches of ¼-inch doweling, or a pencil or a toy wooden rod.

You can disguise your box by giving it a coat of colorful paint.

While it is drying, prepare your wires. With wire cutters or a hacksaw, cut your wire hangers into straight sections of varying lengths. (See picture A.) The longest of the wires should be at least a half inch shorter than the length of your box, and the shortest should be about 4 inches long. You can use from 8 to 12 wirestrings, depending on the size of your box. File both ends of each wire so that they are smooth enough not to irritate the tips of your fingers when you pluck them.

In addition, cut one wire 1½ inches shorter than the width of your box. You need not file it smooth. It is to serve as a crosspiece. At the same time, snip off a piece of lacing of the same size to serve as a cushion for the ends of the strings which are fastened down. Put these two aside together.

When your box is ready to be worked on, place it flat on your work table. About 1½ inches down from the top edge, draw a line leaving an inch margin on each side. (See picture B.) Draw a similar line about ¾ of an inch closer to the center. Then, draw lines every ¾ of an inch crossing your 2 parallel lines. When you are finished, you will have a ladder running across your box.

Where the lines meet, use an awl or a sharp nail to start small holes through the box. Complete drilling the holes you have started with a 3/16th inch or slightly larger bit. (See picture C.)

Now take up your longer piece of lacing or twine. Leave a tail of 6 to 8 inches inside the box to help you later to tighten the cord. Thread in and out of the holes in pairs. (Picture D.) Secure the

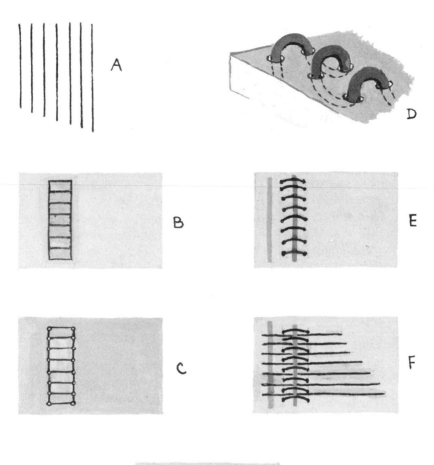

lace on one end, but, for the moment, let the long tail remain untied.

Lay the shorter piece of lacing parallel to the rows of holes and half-way to the same edge of the box. (Picture E.) Take up the special wire also set aside. Slip this through the loops.

Sort your varying lengths of wire and start inserting the longest first. Cushion each on the short lace and slip it under the cross wire. between 2 loops. (Picture F.)

Use a strip of adhesive or masking tape to hold your wires in place while you raise the lid of the box to tighten the loops. Tighten and secure the tail end inside the box but leave room for your dowel or rod to fit underneath the wires.

When the loops are fairly tight, remove the tape and ease the dowel carefully under the wires, as close to the row of loops as possible. (Picture G.)

Prevent the dowel from slipping out of place by drilling a hole in each end through the rod and box top and hammering in a wire brad. Bend the brad over on the inside of the box.

Your wire harp is finished. (See picture, page 95.)

Playing the Harp

Play your harp by pulling down slightly on the end of each wire and letting it go. Let your finger fall onto the board for an added effect. You can play all kinds of rhythms. If you want to make a ladder of sounds, pull the wires in or out a little to adjust the tone to fit your own scale.

Try telling a story, using your harp to make the sound effects.

WASHTUB BASS

You don't need magic to transform an ordinary metal washtub basin into a magnificent bass fiddle. All it takes is a broomstick, a length of clothesline or venetian blind cord and an assortment of hardware — an eye screw, two washers and a nut.

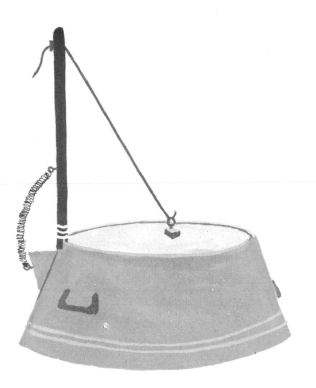

Basin

Use the largest basin or pail you can carry. Turn the washtub upside down. Drill a hole through the center large enough for you to fit in a large screw eye. Cushion the screw with a washer and thread it through. On the inside of the tub, put on another washer and tighten with a nut. Make sure the screw is firmly attached to the basin.

Broomstick

You can leave your broomstick or mop handle its full length. A 3-foot strip of doweling (one inch) would do if necessary. Saw a ¼ to ½-inch notch at the end of the stick so it can fit over the lip of your washtub bottom. Use a chisel to help your saw. Sandpaper the notch smooth. Fit on a brace (you can make it from a coat hanger or similar wire) just above the notch so that the stick won't split.

At a convenient height near the top of the stick, drill a hole large enough so that the clothesline can pass through. As you grow taller, you can make another hole higher up, or if your string is too short, you can add one further down. It will, of course, change the range of sounds. The highest hole will call for the longest cord and make the lowest notes.

Sandpaper your stick smooth. You don't want splinters as a bonus for your playing. Shellac, paint or varnish, if you like.

Adding the String

Tie one end of your clothesline or cord to the screw eye. Thread the other end through the hole of the stick. Then fit the notch on the lip of the basin and hold the stick straight up. Stretch the cord tight and knot the cord on the side of the stick *outside* the basin.

You can cut off some of the excess cord on the other side of the knot but leave a little in case the cord frays at the bottom end and has to be restrung.

Extra Convenience

You can add a spring to attach the handle to the basin so that it will not fall over, but it is not necessary. It requires a wedge so that the spring won't knock against the basin. See picture.

Playing the Bass

To play your bass, stand and rest the basin against your legs. Hold the stick with your left hand and pluck the string with your right. This will be your higher note.

To vary the sounds, tilt the stick toward the center and move your hand down the string (which gets looser) anchoring it to the stick. The lower you move your hand, the shorter the string in use and the lower the note.

If you wear a glove on your right hand, you will avoid the possibility of rope burns as you move up and down the string, and it will not affect the sound.

You can pluck out bass rhythms and, with a little practice, learn to play melodies. The washtub bass makes a fine companion to guitar, banjo, drum and recorder.

CAN CONTRALTO

For the kindergartner in the family, make a smaller version of the washtub bass. You can use a coffee tin or a large fruit juice can. Of course, the music won't be as loud and the range of sounds will be higher. Use a toy rod or pencil as your handle and a steel or piano wire as your string (cord will not make enough sound).

You might even try playing it with a file or make a bow from a dowel stick with strips of fine sandpaper cemented on.

MY-OLIN

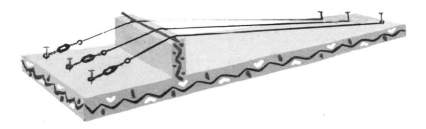

The hardware store will supply most of the simple materials you need to make this rugged stringed instrument. It will stand a good deal of rough treatment and reward efforts to play it with a genuine understanding of the string family of instruments. You can pluck or thump or bow it, and each different way of playing the my-olin makes a different kind of music.

Materials

For the body of your instrument, use wood 2 inches thick, 4 inches wide and about 36 inches long, but the piece of wood need not be regular in outline. An odd shaped strip makes a more attractive instrument.

In addition, you will need a piece of wood 1" x 1" x 4" to act as a stationary bridge, and another ½" x 1" x 1" for a movable bridge to vary the tones.

At the hardware store, pick up 6 heavy large-headed nails (roofing nails or ten penny nails will do), a few light nails and 3 small turnbuckles.

For strings, get steel piano wire of different gauges if possible (13, 15, 19). You don't need more than 3 feet for your lowest string. If you can get very thin wire, you will need less than 2 feet for that string. The thinner the wire, the shorter you should make your string and the higher will be your sound.

If you can get only one size of wire, order about 12 feet for your strings. This will give you a little extra in case a string breaks.

Construction

Drill 3 holes an inch in from one end of your board. These are for fastening the turnbuckles you will use as pegs to tighten the strings. The heavy nails should slip in and out of the holes but should fit fairly closely.

Cut off a small triangle from the bottom end if your wood is symmetrical and you want to vary the shape. Sand your wood smooth. Shellac, varnish or paint if you like — it will not influence the tone.

Bend with pliers or cut with wire cutters a piece of your heaviest wire (perhaps #19 or 20) about 3 inches shorter than the length of your board. Fasten one end to one screw eye of the turnbuckle.

Unscrew the two hooks of the turnbuckle until they are almost completely out so that the turnbuckle is about as long as you can make it.

Slip one heavy nail through the screw eye not attached to the wire and push it into the first hole in your board.

About a half of an inch below the turnbuckle at its longest length, nail the 1" x 1" x 4" bridge strip across the board.

Lay your wire over the bridge and along the length of the board. At a point about an inch from the end, bend the wire as a marker for the loop for the other nail.

If you have a small vise, fasten your nail upright in the vise and using both pliers to grip the wire, wrap it around the nail so as to make a neat loop.

With the loop around its neck, take the nail and stretch the wire along the board. Scratch a mark at the point it reaches. At that point, drill a hole so that the nail will go in up to the head. If the nail comes through on the other side of the wood, cut or saw off the extra length of nail.

You will have plenty of room on the turnbuckle to tighten the wire and get a variety of pitches. If a buzz or rattle persists, cut a piece of coat hanger wire slightly shorter than the width of the board. Loosen the string, slip the hanger wire under the string and across the bridge, and tighten the string on top of it. Try tuning it to low G on the piano or on the violin pitchpipe.

Make each of the strings you put on shorter (and thinner if possible) than the one next to it so that you can stretch each to a higher pitch. With the help of the piano or pitchpipe, you may be able to tune the second string to D and the third to A.

If you get thin enough wire, the last string you put on can be anchored 12 inches from the turnbuckle. Take a look at the strings behind a piano keyboard and see how the shorter wires at the high end are thinner.

Playing the My-olin

Have fun playing the my-olin. Pluck it with a feather quill or hit it with a hammer and listen to the strings vibrate. Take a dull saw or file and rub it back and forth as you would a violin bow. Prop your second strip of wood underneath the strings and play different notes by sliding the bridge back and forth.

VARIATIONS

For Increased Sound

You can increase the volume of your instrument if you cut out a hole in the central portion of the wood 4 or 5 inches long and about 2½ inches wide. Cover this with a scrap of sheepskin or goatskin from the music instrument store.

Soak the skin in COLD water half an hour. Stretch and nail it across the opening with carpet tacks.

To Add a Fourth String

You can make this a four-stringed instrument simply by putting on a fourth string in the same way you put on the other three (make this as thin as you can and tune it to E if possible). But to be able to play it with a bow, it would be better to curve the bridge like this:

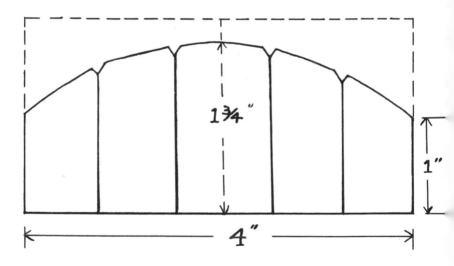

Locate the notches from the strings by laying the flat side A across the board where the turnbuckle holes are drilled, and marking each hole. Draw four straight lines up the curved side B.

My-olin and wire hanger harp (page 86) accompany shakers and light drum. Awaiting attention are rubber hose and copper recorders (page 100), bone rattle, minstrel bones, and tinkle caps.

Make a very slight saw cut (less than ⅛th of an inch) at the four points on the curve.

If the sound is cut down or softened by the bridge, lay a piece of wire, bent slightly to fit the notches, across the top of the bridge under the strings.

10. Blow, Men, Blow

BOTTLE FLUTE

Press the edge of the top of an empty bottle to your lower lip and blow lightly across the top. Pour in a little water and blow again. Your note will be higher.

If you want to add a puzzle to your music making, tap the bottle when it is empty. Then tap again after you've poured in water. Your note will be lower.

KEY WHISTLE

Blow through the opening of a hollow key for strange and eerie sounds.

CORN STALK WHISTLE

Make a whistle from a cornstalk. Cut a 2-inch slit in the stalk from one end. Just below the slit cut out a notch and push the slit piece into the whistle to make a plug.

SODA STRAW PIPE

Link straws of different lengths and whisper "too" into each one. You'll be able to make different sound effects and, with a little practice, even to blow little tunes with your breath.

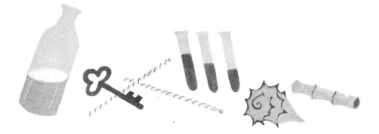

SEA SHELL BLOWER

Make a snail shell into a flute by blowing across the small opening.

Are there other shells you can make into good wind instruments?

PIPES OF PAN

Cut three hollow reeds — Japanese fleece flower, elder, rushes or small cornstalk with joint at one end of each piece. Blow across the hollow tube. The longest pipe will give the lowest tone.

TEST TUBE PIPES

Three test tubes, tuned to different notes with sand, water or clay, make modern Pipes of Pan. Blow, shepherd, blow, but not too hard if you want pleasant notes.

COMB KAZOO

Put your comb to musical use. Fold a piece of waxed or tissue paper in half, and wrap the teeth of the comb in the fold. Put your lips over the paper covering the comb teeth. Be careful not

to get your paper wet. Just hum a tune as you move the comb from side to side. The smaller comb teeth need more effort from you.

HUMBOARD KAZOO

Cover the end of a cardboard tube with an oversized piece of waxed or wrapping paper. Hold the paper tight with a rubber band or a string around the tube, or by pasting it down. Use a nail to punch 8 small round holes an even distance from one another in a straight line along the center of the cardboard tube.

Put your lips to the open end and hum away. Holding your fingers over the holes (as with a flute), you can vary the sounds. Paste on aluminum foil and your humboard will look like a flute.

WILLOW WHISTLE

If you get to a lake, a stream or a pond in the spring, look for a weeping willow tree. That is the time of year to make a willow whistle. The sap will be running, and the bark will be moist and loose.

Break off a branch — and remember that a long whistle makes a deep sound and a short whistle makes a high sound.

There are two different ways to make your whistle. With the second, you may be able to play 3-note tunes.

Johnny One-Note

At one end of your willow branch smooth a place for your lips to go. Notch a piece 2 inches from the mouth end like this:

Tap the bark gently to loosen it, and soak the branch in water. Then slide the bark off all in one piece.

Cut a groove in the wood from the mouth end to the notch, like this:

Slide the bark on again.

Keep the whistle wet and blow. Cut a little more in the same places if it is necessary.

Willow Woodwind

Tap the bark to loosen it and then soak it in water until you can slide it off. Let the bark and the wooden stick dry in the sun.

Push gently on the soft middle part of the bark until it all comes out. Your whistle should be hollow all through.

Cut a little notch about 2 inches from the top. One-fourth of the way from the bottom of the whistle cut a round hole like this:

Then half-way between the first hole and the bottom, cut another hole, like this:

Split a 1-inch piece of the willow wood lengthwise for a little round piece of wood, like this:

Push this into the end of the whistle that you play, like this:

If you like, you can play little tunes. With both holes closed, you have your deepest note. With both holes opened, you play your highest note. Cover the top hole for the middle note.

Whistle away.

RUBBER HOSE RECORDER

With a 12½-inch length of rubber hose, perhaps salvaged from the leaky garden hose, you can make a simple flute or recorder. This will provide a good introduction to the family of wind instruments. Making and mastering a recorder can be a most satisfying musical experience.

The directions here are for a recorder with C as its lowest note. The directions will be exact if your hose diameter measures ⅝ths of an inch inside. A narrow hose recorder will sound slightly higher, and you will have to use a slightly longer hose. A wider hose will sound slightly lower, and you will have to do more snipping with your heavy scissors or tin snips.

THE MOUTHPIECE

Ready-Made Mouthpiece

You can attach the ready-made mouthpiece of a tonette or of a three-penny whistle if it is wide enough to fit tightly either inside or outside the rubber tubing (with the help of friction or adhesive tape if necessary). Your length of rubber hose will be an inch shorter (start with 11½ inches). All other measurements will be the same.

Making a Mouthpiece

To make a mouthpiece, you'll need a one-inch length of dowel (⅝ths of an inch in diameter for ⅝ths-inch hose) to use as a plug.

Before you cut off your inch of dowel, work it into shape. The small piece is hard to anchor in a vise or support with your foot. Use sandpaper or a file and make a flat surface not more than 1/16 of an inch deep and about an inch long, like this:

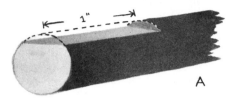

A

Then cut off your one-inch length, and sand the saw cut
smooth. Put your plug aside while you make the notch in your
hose.

One inch down from the top of the hose, chalk a ⅛th-inch
mark on the center of the tube.

With a razor blade or a long-handled hobbyist's knife, make
the ⅛th-inch cut down through the top of the tube.

Starting ¼ of an inch down from the first cut, make a slanting
cut toward the first cut.

Then make two parallel ¼-inch cuts at right angles to the
top cut. (See picture B.)

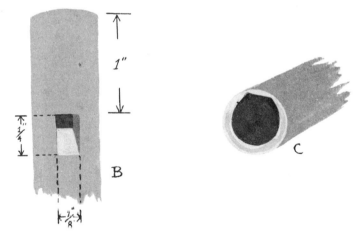

Cut out the excess rubber.

Next, with a small three-cornered file or a narrow but sharp
nail file, file a flat groove ⅛th-inch wide along the inside of the

rubber tubing running straight from the top of the tube down to the notch. (See picture C.)

Fitting the Dowel Plug

Fit your wooden plug into the rubber hose until the inside edge of the dowel comes just in line with the cut in the rubber tube. The flat side of the dowel should be just under the flat groove of the tube.

Blow gently. It should play sweetly. If it doesn't, push the plug out with a thin stick and file the flat groove down a little.

If the tone sounds very thin, try making the hole in the tubing a little wider than the ⅛th-inch.

Variation

For less flexible tubing (plastic, aluminum, copper or bamboo) use cork or balsa wood for the plug. Also, cut a section for your lips, like this:

In place of tin snips, use a coping saw or hacksaw for the bamboo and a hacksaw for the plastic, aluminum or copper.

MAKING THE RECORDER

Check the note you can blow in tune with the C above middle C on a piano, a C pitchpipe or tuning fork. Snip off a little at a time from the bottom until your C sounds right. You will probably have a 12-inch hose.

The next step is to locate holes at the right spots. Starting at the bottom end, measure up 2 inches for the first hole and mark the spot with a chalk line one inch long. Make other chalk marks similarly at the points noted in Pictures A and B (page 104).

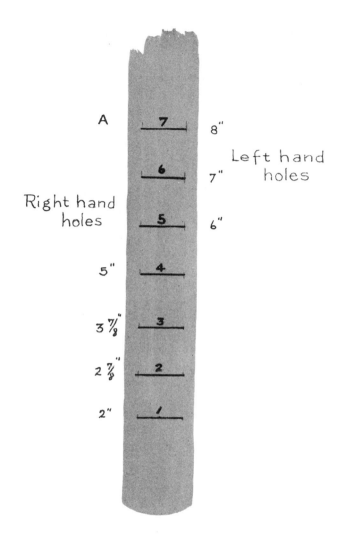

Now place your fingers on the marks you have made. If you are right-handed, your left hand should be nearest the mouthpiece. The top mark (#7) should be covered by your left index finger. One-half inch below will be your left thumb hole (#8) on the

B

8" ———— $7\frac{1}{2}$"

Left thumb
on underside

underside of the hose. Middle and ring fingers rest on marks #6 and #5. Don't use the little finger of your left hand. See Picture C for the right hand positions. Notice that you use the right little finger but not your right thumb.

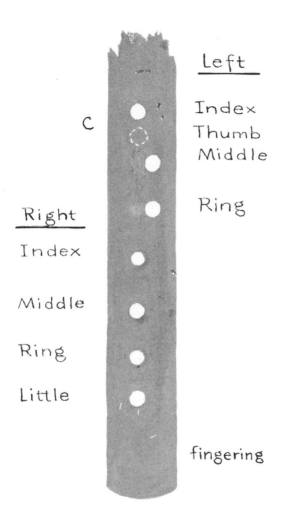

C

Index
Thumb
Middle

Ring

Right

Index

Middle

Ring

Little

fingering

At each spot where your finger falls naturally, chalk in a crossing line. They need *not* be in a straight line (See Picture D.)

Pinpoint the holes at the centers of the crossmarks with an awl or sharpened nail and finish boring with a ¼-inch hand drill

To correct any mistakes, you can take a small round file and

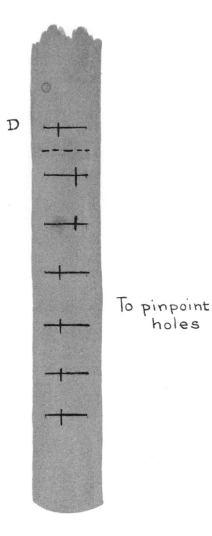

D

To pinpoint
holes

work the hole down toward the bottom of the hose (if the pitch is too high) or work it upwards (if the pitch is too low). If a hole gets too large, cover part of it with tape or cover it completely if necessary.

The hole should be sanded smooth by rolling the sandpaper tightly and sanding along the outside of the hose. This will hollow out a curved place for your fingers to fit more easily in playing.

You now have a very personal instrument made to fit your hands alone. The next job is learning how to play your recorder.

Playing the Recorder

Don't expect to master your recorder immediately. But it will be well worth the time and effort it will take to learn to play. The fingering is the same as that used on a wood recorder and on any copper, aluminum, bamboo or plastic recorders you make.

Keep your lips toward the tip of the mouthpiece. Blow gently for the low notes and harder for the higher sounds.

FINGERING

Start with your left hand, nearest the mouthpiece. (See Picture C.)

> D — all holes open
> C — cover #7 (index finger)
> B — cover #7 and #8 (index and thumb)
> A — cover #8, #7 and #6 (thumb, index and middle)
> G — cover #8, #7, #6 and #5 (entire left hand except little finger)

Practice the left hand for a time. When you are sure of it, add your right hand. Your right hand is *never* used without your left hand.

> F — #4 (right index)
> E — #4 and #2 and #1 (right index, ring and little — ONLY RIGHT MIDDLE OFF)
> D — #4, #2 and #3 (index, middle and ring — ONLY LITTLE FINGER OFF)
> C — cover all holes (lowest note on recorder)

Higher Scale

To play the same scale an octave higher, press the tip of your thumb into #8, covering only half the hole. Use the same fingers for the various notes.

Sharps and Flats for the Recorder

Here's how to raise the pitch just a little to play a sharp or lower it just a little for a flat.

You play A by closing holes #8, #7 and #6 (left thumb, index and middle fingers). To make G, one note lower, you cover one more hole (with your left ring finger). But to play A flat, you cover the three holes for A, then leave #5 open, and cover the hole #4 (right index). That lowers the pitch slightly.

For a sharp, do the same thing in reverse. Remember, a flatted note is the same as the sharped note below it. E flat is the same as D sharp. D flat is the same as C sharp.

A Song to Play

Even if you are not complete master of your recorder, try playing this simple tune.

		AA					
	GG		G				
				FF			
					EE		
						DD	
CC							C

Twinkle	Twinkle	Little	Star	How I	Wonder	What You	Are
cover all	left hand	left thumb, index, middle	left hand	left hand, right index	only right middle off	only left little off	cover all

```
GG                                      GG
      FF                                      FF
            EE                                      EE
                  D                                       D
Up a-bove the world so high             Like a diamond in the sky

left    left    only    only            left    left    only only
hand    hand,   right   left            hand    hand,   right left
        right   middle  little                  right   middle little
        index   off     off                     index   off   off

                  AA
      GG                  G               FF
                                                EE
                                                      DD
CC                                                          C
Twinkle Twinkle Little Star         How I Wonder What You Are
```

BASS RUBBER HOSE RECORDER

You can make a rubber hose recorder an octave lower than the one described. Just cut your length of rubber hose to about 2 feet. You will probably snip off 2 inches to raise the pitch in tune. Check it with low C on the piano.

The first hole will be about 2 inches from the bottom of the hose. The other holes will be a little farther apart than those in Pictures A and B on pages 103 and 104. The distances will depend on the whistle mouthpiece and the smoothness of the inside hole. The lower notes will have to be played very softly.

PAPOOSE PIPE

If the small member of the family insists on blowing on an instrument, too, you might make a 3-note pipe for him as your gift. The recorder fingering may be too complicated for the pre-

• **Blow, Men, Blow** • 109

school child. This simpler instrument will resemble your recorder and be much easier to handle.

For Solos

You will need a piece of rubber hose at least 6 inches long. Shorter than that will make an instrument too shrill to be pleasant.

Fit on a tonette or three-penny whistle mouthpiece tightly or make a mouthpiece. (See page 101.)

Pinpoint 2 holes with a nail anywhere in the bottom half of the pipe. Then finish boring with a ¼-inch hand drill. Sand the holes smooth.

For Duets

If you want to be able to play duets on the papoose pipe and the recorder, make sure the papoose pipe measures 12½ inches. After the mouthpiece is ready, tune the pipe to the Middle C on the piano or on your recorder by snipping off a little at a time. Make your first hole 2 inches from the bottom and your second hole ⅞ths of an inch higher up.

Play the pipe with whatever fingers are comfortable.

C — both holes closed
D — #2 closed
E — both open

Try this simple 3-note song on your Papoose Pipe.

E   E
 D   D
  C   C
Hot cross buns   Hot cross buns

            E
     D D D D D
C C C C   C
One a penny Two a penny Hot cross buns

Try blowing softly, as well as loudly.

11. Clay

To make musical instruments of clay, you will need the use of a kiln, an oven that fires clay to a red heat to harden it. The smaller kilns are moderate in price and many community centers and schools are now equipped with them for their arts and crafts programs. Otherwise, the local pottery, art supply store or perhaps brickyard may have a kiln that you can arrange to use for a small fee.

Possibly the best material for the beginner is low-firing red clay, which remains pliable for a longer time and looks good without glazing (the glass coating with which earthenware is often colored and decorated). You can buy red plastic clay from a mail order house, art supply store, local brickyard or, in some areas, dig it up in the backyard. It would be wise when you buy your clay also to buy a small quantity of dry powdered clay to convert into slip (liquid clay) to use as glue.

With these supplies, you can make a drum, bell, rattle, panpipe and an ocarina or clay flute.

TIPS ON CLAY

1. Always find out the firing temperature of clay when you buy it.

2. Most clay is wrapped well and ready to use when opened. If your clay is too sticky, let it stand on absorbent paper toweling or newspaper a few minutes. Then knead it a bit with your fingers

and let it stand again. Repeat this process until the clay no longer sticks to your fingers.

3. Store clay in a tightly covered container which will not rust.

4. Wedge your clay to avoid air bubbles which will cause cracking in firing, by cutting the clay, then pounding or kneading it.

5. Always start your clay molding by rolling the clay into a ball with the palms of your hands.

6. If the clay gets too hard while you are working with it, moisten it a bit with water.

7. Once your clay is leather hard, mend it with moist rags and thick slip (liquid clay).

8. Clay shrinks as it dries and in firing.

9. Old, dried-out clay should be converted to slip by soaking in water in a sealed container.

CLAY DRUM

Put aside a mixing bowl (plastic will do) to use as a form.

Make a ball and from that a flat pancake. Then use the slab method. Place a piece of oilcloth, rough side up, on your table, and put the clay over that. Then take 2 rulers or similar slats of wood and place one on either side of your clay. This will enable you to roll the clay out evenly. With a rolling pin, tall glass or a length of 1-inch doweling, roll a pie crust of clay about ¼ of an inch thick.

Lift the clay by holding the edges of the cloth on which it has been lying. Carefully drape it into the mixing bowl. Smooth out any cracks. Run your knife along the edges, trimming off the excess clay. Form a little ridge about the mouth of the shell. First prick around the edge with a knife, then put on a little water or slip (liquid clay) and finally press on a tiny coil of clay. Weld the coil on smoothly, allowing no cracks to remain. Make sure the edges are smooth so that they will not cut the drumhead when it is attached.

Carefully poke out 4 holes on one side of the drum body. You will later use these for wire loops (fastened inside) with which to suspend the drum from a rack.

If you want to attach your drumhead by lacing it to the body (Method #4 on page 114), prepare to do so by punching holes toward the bottom of the shell. If you place the holes in an even row, they may weaken the shell. Instead, stagger them up and down, and perhaps make an interesting pattern. Be sure the edges of the holes are very smooth. (After the shell has dried, sandpaper them if necessary.)

Drying

Then put your drum frame aside to dry. Allow it to remain in the form from half an hour to 2 or 3 hours, depending on the weather. When it is leather hard, still wet but too stiff to bend, carefully remove the shell from the form. It should come away from the oilcloth easily since clay shrinks as it dries. If any particles of oilcloth stick, they will burn away in the oven.

Put the drum aside to finish drying in a cool, dry place. It will take several days to a week.

When it is bone dry, smooth and round off all sharp edges with fine sandpaper.

It is ready for the kiln.

Decorating

During the period when the drum is leather hard, you may carve in designs with a pencil-sized pointed stick. DON'T glaze the drumshell; a glaze cuts the resonance of the drum.

If you want to color the shell, wait until the firing is completed. Then paint it in one or more bright water colors. Allow it to dry, and then apply a coat of shellac.

Preparing the Skin

You will need a skin 2 to 4 inches larger in diameter than the diameter of your drumshell. See page 57 for preparations. DON'T punch holes in the skin unless you are using Methods #3 or #4 (see below) of attaching the drumhead.

Attaching the Drumhead

#1   Secure the drumhead to the drumshell by winding heavy twine or thongs cut from raw skinhide just below the ridge of the frame. Get someone to help you by stretching the skin very tightly while you tighten the string.

#2   Have someone hold the skin tight while you make a hoop of coat hanger wire just below the ridge of the frame. Wind the ends about one another. Keep turning the twisted ends with a pair of pliers until they are tight enough.

#3   See page 64 for coconut ring method of attaching drumhead.

#4   See page 73 for the stovepipe hole-lace method.

CLAY BELL

Bells may be made by a modified pinch bowl method. It would be well to remember that a thin bell will make a clear tone, and the thinner and wider the bell, the deeper the sound.

Make a ball of clay about the size of a golf ball by rolling the clay between your palms. Hold the ball in the palm of one hand and push the thumb of your other hand into the center until it is ¼ of an inch from the bottom. Gradually widen the opening until it is about 3 inches in diameter, and the thickness of the entire piece is about ¼ of an inch. Place the clay into a cup or rounded jelly jar (sprinkled with talcum to prevent sticking) and finish molding the bell in the form. Leave it in the form for 15 minutes or half an hour.

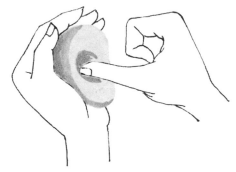

Then make a handle with which to hang the bell. With a knife, prick the top of the bell at 2 places about ¾ of an inch apart. Be sure to coat the pricks with water or liquid clay. Roll a 3 or 4 inch coil. Hold a pencil or toy rod over the center of the bell between the 2 places pricked and form your handle around it (see picture). Join the handle. Weld on the two ends of the handle.

On the side of the bell, attach in the same way a 1-inch coil to form a ring from which to attach the clapper of the bell.

Roll a little ball and elongate it slightly (see picture). Punch a hole just large enough for a thin wire to go through.

Leave the bell and separate clapper in a cool, dry place for several days to a week.

When it is bone dry, smooth it down with fine sandpaper if necessary. Tap the bell with a pencil or very carefully try out your clapper. If you care to raise the tone, sandpaper the lower edge. To lower the tone, sandpaper inside. Be sure to separate the bell and clapper BEFORE you fire them.

It is now ready to fire.

Decorating

If you glaze the bell, be sure you apply a very thin glaze. DON'T GLAZE the clapper.

You may water color and shellac.

CLAY MARACAS

Making a maracas is a simple clay project. You will need some old newspaper to serve as a base.

Before you shape the maracas, prepare the "corn" or "rice" which will move about inside to make the rattle. Just roll about 2 dozen tiny balls of clay. Wrap each one separately in several layers of newspaper.

Pile your paper-covered balls of clay together and wrap the entire mass in a large sheet of newspaper. You will have to cover this with several more layers of newspaper until you have a ball about 3 inches in diameter. Put this aside for the minute.

Roll your clay into a ball and make a pancake of it. Then lay it on a strip of oilcloth between 2 rulers or sticks. Use a rolling pin or 1-inch dowel to roll it out, going from the center first to one end and then to the other. Keep rolling until your clay is about ½-inch thick.

Then carefully lift it by holding onto the two edges of oilcloth and mold it around your ball of newspapers. It should come off the oilcloth cleanly. Leave a ½-inch opening at one point for your handle. As the maracas is fired, the paper will burn away leaving the inside hollow and the clay "corn" free to rattle around.

For the handle, roll a coil about ½-inch thick (see picture). With a knife, prick lines like tire treads on the ball on either side of the opening. Wet the lines with water or liquid clay and weld on the handle. Be sure there are no cracks.

At a point near the bottom of the ball, punch a small hole. Otherwise, air will be trapped inside and the maracas will break while it is being fired.

Lay the instrument aside to dry for 3 days to a week. It is now ready for the kiln.

Decorating

Paint with oil paints or water color and then shellac.

12. How to Make Like a Musician

Once your instruments are made, come away from your workbench to further adventure in the world of sound. Play and work at the game of making music. Experiment, explore, learn and enjoy.

Each instrument has a different timbre — a special coloring or character of its own. Don't take any instrument for granted. Try new ways of making music with it. Perhaps the old ways will prove better, but perhaps not.

Drum

Play a drum on its sides, edges, center, off-center. Use your fingers, your palms, your fists, a straight stick, a softbeater, a hard thumper. Hit it hard; hit it soft. Beat it fast; beat it slow. Put your hand on the head to feel it move or vibrate or to muffle the sound as you play. Parade as you play. Dance as you play. Sing as you play. Combine with a lighter drum and beat part of your rhythm on one drum and part on the second drum.

My-olin

Tighten one string of the mv-olin. Listen to it get higher and higher. Tighten it until it breaks. Tune each string to various notes. Pound the board with a hammer. Pluck the strings with a feather quill. Play one string with a violin bow. Pick two strings together and learn about chords. Play the my-olin across your lap. Play it standing up. Play it from the floor. Beat time with it. Sing with it. Tell your own song stories with it. Get together with someone who can play the washtub bass or rubber hose recorder.

Rattle

Shake a rattle up and down. Shake it in a circle. Tap it gently with the tips of the fingers. Use one rattle; use two rattles. Hit the handle of one with the handle of the other. Shake a rattle to a phonograph record, to the radio, to TV music. Dance with a rattle. Sing with a rattle. Try playing it with a marimba.

Your Job

Can you think of more ways to use these instruments? What about the others you have made?

THE BAND OR ORCHESTRA

How do we make music together?

To begin, choose simple music with a strong rhythm. A folk tune is perhaps best. There are inexpensive paper-backed folk song books which are an excellent source of familiar material.

Be sure everyone knows the piece you decide on. Let the players sit in a group with their instruments beside them while one of the melody instruments plays it through or those familiar with the song sing it or a phonograph recording is put on.

You might go through the number once clapping the rhythm — heavy and light, fast and slow. The heaviest beat or accent falls on the first beat of the pattern.

Gradually a few of the rhythm instruments can start experimenting, and eventually each of the players can join in. Discuss together any sections calling for particular instruments.

Orchestrating

Then try to work out the best arrangement or orchestration for the song. Each of the players might take a turn as orchestrator-conductor, deciding which instruments are to play during the various parts of the music. The choice of instruments at a particular portion might depend on how loud you want it to be, on a particular sound effect desired or on whether you want happy or sad sounds, fast or slow rhythm, low or high tones.

Group your rhythm instruments as to heavy, medium or light. For most music, try to have more light instruments than loud ones or the loud ones will be the only ones heard. Remember, though, that the method of playing can convert a heavy instrument to a light one. Place similar instruments together to make conducting easier.

If you have any melody instruments, arrange them in front. You can use any of those you have made — recorder, flower pot bell set, marimba, fiber pipe drums, washtub bass, musical glasses. Of course, you can substitute a piano or a recording.

Keep some of the rhythm instruments playing throughout to maintain the beat, but don't drown out the melody instruments by having too much rhythm going on at the same time. Try to use all the instruments at least once and perhaps fit in a solo or two or a duet.

The conductor's job is not merely to beat time, but also to point with a "come in" signal to the instruments he wants to play

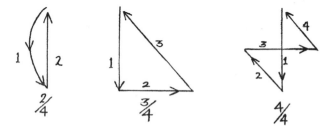

Hand motions for beating time

and a "drop out" signal to those he wants to be quiet. He can raise his hand high for loud playing and lower his hand for the group to play softly. You can develop your own signals.

Start

Low

Loud

"You play"

Stop

SAMPLE "ACCUMULATION" ARRANGEMENT

This arrangement which starts small and gets bigger and louder gives the effect of approaching from a distance.

"SHE'LL BE COMING ROUND THE MOUNTAIN"

PHRASE 1 and 2: She'll be coming round the mountain when she comes,
She'll be coming round the mountain when she comes

Instruments:	Piano or phonograph (softly), rubber hose recorders, stringed instruments, one light hand drum, any very light instruments
PHRASE 3 and 4:	She'll be comin' round the mountain She'll be comin' round the mountain . . .
Instruments:	Those in phrase 1 and 2, plus shakers, rattles, heavier sounding drum
PHRASE 5 and 6:	She'll be comin' round the mountain, She'll be comin' round the mountain when she comes
Instruments:	All the heavy sounding drums, sticks, and any other instruments. Have everyone start this section playing rather softly but with each phrase getting a little louder until at the end everyone is blasting away as loudly as possible.

Other Possibilities

The sample arrangement started with a few instruments and gradually brought in the whole band. You can reverse the order and drop out instruments one by one until finally only a flower pot or a soft recorder is playing.

You can also play the piece faster and faster starting slowly at the beginning.

INSTRUMENTS WITH MAKE-BELIEVE

Make your instruments part of your playacting and shows. They can make fine contributions for solos, dance accompaniment, sound effects or background music.

Take them along on your cowboy rides — a Chinese wood block makes spirited galloping horses. Cowboy songs do better with banjo, my-olin or wire hanger harp. Indian messages travel by tom-tom, and Indian war dances are more fearsome with angry drums.

Your Mexican puppets need maracas, claves, castanets, sand-blocks and possibly a marimba for their dances.

What would an old-fashioned minstrel show be without banjos and bones as well as straw hats?

Are you Casey Jones? Where are your whistles? A ballet dancer? How can you dance without music? A woodsman? There's no sound of an axe?

INSTRUMENT GAMES FOR TWO OR MORE
RHYTHM MIMES

When two or more get together, try this fast moving rhythm game.

Collect enough instruments for each of you except one. Fill in with "Odds and Ends" (page 76) if you do not have enough. Draw lots for the instruments. The one with the blank sheet is "it."

"It" claps a rhythm. Each of the others tries to reproduce the rhythm on the instrument he has drawn — drum, tambourine, rattle, jingle clog, wire harp, recorder, etc.

First to miss becomes "it" for the next round. If no one misses, "it" is still "it" — and he better make the rhythm harder.

GUESS THE SONG

Again instruments are distributed by lot. Each player, in turn, taps out the rhythm of a well-known song and the others try to guess the name.

The group may split into teams and tap out rhythms as a band while the other team guesses. Ten points allowed to a team that guesses correctly, but a point is subtracted for each wrong guess before the correct one is given. First team to get 100 points wins — perhaps the right to order a concert from the losing team.

INSTRUMENT CHARADES

Have an assortment of instruments available (look to "Odds and Ends" again if necessary), but there need be no specific number. A large variety will make for a more interesting game.

Each player decides what he will imitate. Possible choices: horse galloping, train pulling out, roller skating, ticking clock, marching soldier, running water, Indian war dance, Chinese wedding, etc.

The player may select whatever instrument — or instruments — he wishes. The listener who guesses first plays next. If there are enough players, divide into bands, write down assignments and have the players of opposing bands draw for turns.

The guessing must be done by the band whose player is performing. Just to add spice, the guessing might be in the form of pantomime, the guessing individual silently acting to the music so that his own band can put the music and action into words.

BUTTON, BUTTON WHO PLAYED WHAT

Again draw for instruments (no melody instruments this time), and the one who draws an empty paper is "It."

"It" leaves the room. The others form a circle with an instrument beside each player. The group decides on a rhythm and, if It is a large group, also chooses an arranger.

"It" returns and stands in the center of the circle. While "It" is facing elsewhere the arranger (outside the circle) taps one player to play a solo. When "It" turns, the arranger taps another instrument to take up the rhythm. "It" must catch a player while he is playing. The fun depends on the rhythm never being lost, even during the change of instrumentalist.

SIMPLE SIMON PLAYS

The leader has two instruments (the game is harder with two drums or two rattles). One instrument is "Simple." If Simple does it, the other instrumentalists do it. If the leader's other instrument plays, no one else does. Anyone who plays at the wrong time is out.

INDEX

American Indian Morache, 14-15
Ball Beater, 53
Balloon Babbler, 25
Band Box Drum, 76
Barrel Conga, 58
Barrel Rack, 74
Bars, 29
Basket Drum, 48
Basket Stem Bell, 79
Bass Rubber Hose Recorder, 109
Bead Beater, 53
Bell Bracelets, 34
Bell Stick, 34
Bells, 34-42, 78, 79, 115-116
Bone Rattle, 18-19
Bottle Flute, 96
Bottle Prattle, 25
Box Banjo, 84
Brad Bells, 78
Brass Cymbals, 31
Brass Rod Chimes, 37
Brass Tube Triangle, 29
Brave Drum, 46-47
Button Ankle Rattles, 79
Button, Button Who Played What, 125
Can Contralto, 91
Cap Tinkles, 31
Cardboard Bell Tambourine, 50
Cardboard Maracas, 25
Castanets, 27-28, 78
Cheesebox Hoop, 49
Cheesebox Hoop Tambourine, 51
Chair Rack, 74
Chimes, 37-39
Chinese Wood Block, 13
City Slicker Sticks, 9
Claves, 10
Clay Bell, 115-116
Clay Drum, 112-114
Clay Instruments, 111-117
Clay Maracas, 116-117
Clothespin Chatterboxes, 17
Coat Button Castanets, 78
Coat Hanger Triangle, 29

Coconut Bongos, 65
Coconut Drums, 62
Coconut Halves, 14
Comb Kazoo, 97
Corn Stalk Whistle, 96
Country Style Sticks, 10
Curved Thumper, 55
Cymbals, 30-31
Dowel Drumstick, 54
Drum Set Frame, 73
Drums, 44-75, 78, 112-114, 118
Drumsticks, 52-56
Fiber Pipe Drum Set, 67
Flower Pot Bells, 35
Grater Guayo, 15
Guess the Song, 124
Guiro, 15
Horseshoe Triangle, 29
Hot Tin Can, 79
Humboard Kazoo, 98
Instrument Charades, 125
Instrument Games, 124-126
Jangle Ring, 33
Jingle Clogs, 32-33
Jingle Ring, 24
Johnny One-Note, 98
Kettle Drum, 78
Key Whistle, 96
Kitchenware Cymbals, 30
Makeshift Cymbals, 30
Maracas, 19, 77, 116-117
Marimbas, 39-43
Medicine Man Water Drum, 47-48
Minstrel Bones, 10-11
Mixing Bowl Drum, 48
Moraches, 14-15
Musical Glasses, 38-39
My-olin, 91-95, 118
Nail Chimes, 37
Nature Walk Cymbals, 30
Notched Stick, 11
One-Octave Marimba, 42-43
Orchestrating, 120-123
Paper Bag Maracas, 77
Papier-Mache Knob, 54

Papoose Pipe, 109
Papoose Tomtom, 44-45
Pencil Stick, 53
Pie Pan Tambourine, 50
Pipes of Pan, 97
Plywood Guiros, 15
Pop Top Castanets, 19
Pot Cover Gong, 79
Rattles, 16-26, 79, 119
Rhythm Band, 118-123
    Odds and ends for, 76-81
Rhythm Blocks, 12-14
Rhythm Mimes, 124
Rhythm Sticks, 9-11
Rubber Hose Recorder, 100-110
Salt Box Drum, 76
Sandpaper Blocks, 12
Sandpaper Sticks, 14
Scrapers, 14-15, 17, 77
Scraping Screw, 77
Sea Shell Blower, 97
Shakers, 16-18
Shoebox Strummer, 84
Shoe Shine Shaker, 24
Shoetree Thumper, 53
Short Pipe Drum, 72
Simple Simon, 126
Skin Drumheads, 57
Skin Drums, 57-76
Sleigh Bells, 34
Slingshot Strummer, 83
Soda Straw Pipe, 96
Softened Thumper, 55
Special Clog Handles, 32
Spoon Syncopators, 80

Square Frame, 74
Squaw Tomtom, 45-46
Stone Bells, 36
Stove Pipe Drum, 71
String Bass, 78
Strings, 78, 82-95
Tambourines, 50-52, 80
Temporary Tambourine, 80
Ten-Penny Triangle, 77
Tennis Ball Racket, 25
Test Tube Pipes, 97
Three-Note Marimba, 41
Tin Can Tomtoms, 44-48
Tin Can Tubo, 16
Tin Clinkers, 31
Toy Box Marimba, 40
Train Bells, 35
Tree Thumper, 55
Triangle Forks, 80
Triangles, 28-29, 77, 80
Tuber Harp, 82
Turkey Drumstick, 53
Urban Slingshot Strummer, 83
Variable Pitch Coconut Drum, 65-67
Walnut Castanets, 28
Washboard Morache, 14
Washtub Bass, 88-91
Whisk Broom Brush, 54
Whisk Broom Swish, 80
Willow Whistle, 98-100
Willow Woodwind, 99
Wind Instruments, 96-110
Wire Hanger Harp, 86-88
Wishbone Harp, 82
Wooden Spoon Rhythm, 80